PRAISE FOR ↴

"*Rooted & Rising: Voices of Courage in a Time of Climate Crisis* is a true gem. Filled with inspiring personal stories, contemplations on how to live with honesty and compassion in the midst of climate disruption, thoughtful questions for the reader to consider, and creative rituals to access our deepest emotional responses to the climate crisis, this book is a must-read for anyone and everyone who cares about planet Earth and all of its inhabitants."
—Rabbi Katy Z. Allen, eco-chaplain, founder of Ma'yan Tikvah—A Wellspring of Hope, and co-founder of Jewish Climate Action Network

"This timely book is not about overcoming climate change—it's about climate activism as a devotional practice. It's about honoring God, the Oneness that flows through everything. It's about building community and loving our neighbors (including the whole natural world) and feeding the hungry and protecting the poor. It's about the meaning of faith and about responding with all of our hearts and souls and might to meet the needs of this Climate era. It will motivate you and your communities to live as citizens of one earth."
—Rabbi Ellen Bernstein, The Promise of the Land: A Passover Haggadah; Founder, Shomrei Adamah, Keepers of the Earth, first national Jewish environmental organization

"Whatever your faith or spiritual background, this provocative collection of essays will stimulate new thought and action. This book is for everyone who has been frustrated by the lack of progress in addressing climate change. These pages will educate and inspire you and renew your strength." —The Rev. Canon Sally Bingham, Founder and President Emeritus Interfaith Power and Light

"This book does more than sound the alarm about the ecological destruction we have wrought and the catastrophic doom that awaits. Sound the alarm it does. But most importantly, it leads us to think deeply about how we sustain ourselves and the rest of our sacred Creation after the alarm has been sounded. Through passionate storytelling, this book shares a wellspring of faith practices and inner resources that sustain readers in moments of despair and lead them to a place of hope in the midst of a terminal climate crisis. The strength, wisdom, and reservoir of faith that fill these pages inspire one to take action to save our Creation. And so, for all who sometimes feel hopeless but refuse to give up on ourselves and our earthly home, this book is a must-read. It provides you with the 'stuff' to continue in the struggle to 'midwife whatever new life will be born out of this cataclysmic time.'" —The Very

Rev. Dr. Kelly Brown Douglas, Dean, Episcopal Divinity School at Union Theological Seminary, and author, *Stand Your Ground: Black Bodies and the Justice of God*

"Leah D. Schade and Margaret Bullitt-Jonas have gathered the spiritual and practical wisdom we need for such a time as this. As ministers, activists, and scholars, they know we must take bold action that heals the land, the waters, the skies, and the whole family of God. They also know our faith traditions provide us with the fuel we need. I hope people of faith everywhere will open this book, explore the diverse and rich collection of voices, and be encouraged, challenged, informed, strengthened, rooted and driven to prayer and action." —The Most Rev. Michael B. Curry, Presiding Bishop, The Episcopal Church

"*Rooted and Rising* is a deeply personal series of essays by those who see climate activism as a calling. At a time when the challenge may seem insurmountable, this book is a celebration of community. These essays show us that doing the work becomes its own end, and that the fulfillment we find in each other and in nature nourishes and sustains us in the struggle." —Nicole Ghio, Friends of the Earth

"*Rooted and Rising* should be required reading at all Christian seminaries, rabbinical colleges, and Islamic colleges! Leah D. Schade and Margaret Bullitt-Jonas have successfully made the case for a critical engagement in climate justice and ethical sustainability. This collection of essays and interviews provides an important way forward for religious leaders to take action using the best sources in their own religious traditions while cultivating interfaith friendships to work for eco-justice." —David Grafton, Professor of Islamic Studies and Christian-Muslim Relations, Hartford Theological Seminary

"Huge problems—war, poverty, civil rights—experienced serious progress in America only after the religious community got committed. Just in time for the 50th anniversary of Earth Day, *Rooted and Rising* provides a powerful spiritual and moral case for people of faith becoming involved in climate activism." —Denis Hayes, founder of The Earth Day Network

"In the face of an absolute emergency, the voices in *Rooted and Rising* represent an important source of inspiration and challenge. There is no time left for delay or half-heartedness in our response to the climate crisis, and these authors call on all of us to do everything we can for the sake of our precious planet." —The Rev. Fletcher Harper, Executive Director, GreenFaith

"Earth's shared spaces impose on us shared responsibilities. The imminent collapse of Earth's systems make it imperative that we think and work together to reverse these life-threatening processes. This volume draws copiously from the deep well of the Abrahamic traditions and shows us how this work can be done." —Fazlun Khalid, Founder/Director, Islamic Foundation for Ecology and Environmental Sciences

"If you're part of the 'choir' regarding climate change, if you get it, if you're on board, this is the book you need right now. It will help you keep singing, even when politicians and corporate leaders prove themselves bigger fossil fools than before, even when the news is bleaker, even when you lose hope for the tenth time, but still can't give up. This book put new steel in my spine and fired up my resolve. You need this book, and the Earth needs you to take its message and resources to heart." —Brian D. McLaren, author/speaker/ activist

"It is now clear: prophetic, spiritual resilience in the face of the Earth emergency is indispensable to our health and a catalyst for any eco-social transformation we might muster. In *Rooted & Rising*, climate activists beneath the Abrahamic canopy—Jews, Muslims, Christians—voice exactly what we need and show the way. Kudos to Leah D. Schade and Margaret Bullitt-Jonas for convening this remarkable gathering and offering spiritual practices to accompany the inspiring witness." —Larry Rasmussen, Reinhold Niebuhr Professor of Social Ethics, Union Theological Seminary

"This important book is a collection of wise testimonies about how people of different spiritual backgrounds sustain their grit amid the climate crisis: they release false idols, practice truth-telling, grieve, lament, breathe, pray, practice gratitude, embrace community, and live out their faith by taking action. I laughed, cried, and knowingly sighed as I identified with the experiences of these diverse climate justice leaders." —Shantha Ready Alonso, Executive Director, Creation Justice Ministries

"Hope flows, aided by spirit; fear and grief must be named and honored; resilience and justice are within us; holy paradoxes abound, as people of faith confront our climate-imperiled era. These are just a few of the vital messages delivered in this poignant, timely, diverse collection. I'll be returning to *Rooted and Rising* often, and anticipate that many others will, too." —Rabbi Fred Scherlinder Dobb, Adat Shalom, Bethesda, MD; Chair, Coalition on the Environment and Jewish Life

"This stunning collection of essays is like nothing we have seen before. With its honest acknowledgement of the raw fear, anger, and despair evoked by the climate crisis, *Rooted and Rising* will take readers to places they have never been—but which they need to face. At the same time, the book lifts up something equally real: the extraordinary power of human beings to take collective action, if they so choose. *Rooted and Rising* shows how claiming our relationship with all of life is the foundation of spirituality (with or without religious faith); how the energy of our feelings can be turned into positive action; and how our lives can find purpose and meaning in this perilous time."
—Lise Van Susteren, M.D., co-author of *The Psychological Effects of Global Warming on the United States: And Why the U.S. Mental Health Care System Is Not Adequately Prepared* and *Emotional Inflammation*

"By now there are many books about global scorching and the climate crisis, but this one is unusual—perhaps unique. All the contributors explore their own personal trajectories toward understanding and acting on the danger in first-person, not third-person, mode. Even theological journeys are presented as actual journeys by the writers, not only as assertions about holy text. And at the end of each section of the book are exercises to invite the reader into the same kind of personal journey. The result is both enlivened and enlivening." —Rabbi Arthur Waskow, director of The Shalom Center; author of *Godwrestling: Round 2* and *Down-to-Earth Judaism*

Rooted and Rising

Rooted and Rising

Voices of Courage in a Time of Climate Crisis

Leah D. Schade and
Margaret Bullitt-Jonas, editors

ROWMAN & LITTLEFIELD
Lanham • Boulder • New York • London

Published by Rowman & Littlefield
An imprint of The Rowman & Littlefield Publishing Group, Inc.
4501 Forbes Boulevard, Suite 200, Lanham, Maryland 20706
www.rowman.com

6 Tinworth Street, London SE11 5AL, United Kingdom

British Library Cataloguing in Publication Information Available

Library of Congress Cataloging-in-Publication Data

Names: Schade, Leah D., author. | Bullitt-Jonas, Margaret, author.
Title: Rooted and rising : voices of courage in a time of climate crisis /
    Leah D. Schade and Rev. Dr. Margaret Bullitt-Jonas.
Description: Lanham : Rowman & Littlefield, [2019] | Includes
    bibliographical references and index. | Summary: "Rooted and Rising is
    an edited volume intended for readers who are concerned about the
    climate crisis and who thirst for the wisdom and spiritual resources of
    fellow pilgrims grappling with despair"—Provided by publisher.
Identifiers: LCCN 2019020405 (print) | LCCN 2019980391 (ebook) | ISBN
    9781538127759 (cloth : alk. paper) | ISBN 9781538127766 (pbk. : alk.
    paper) | ISBN 9781538127773 (ebook)
Subjects: LCSH: Climatic changes—Religious aspects. | Human
    ecology—Religious aspects. | Ecology—Religious aspects.
Classification: LCC QC903 .S33 2019 (print) | LCC QC903 (ebook) | DDC
    201/.77—dc23
LC record available at https://lccn.loc.gov/2019020405
LC ebook record available at https://lccn.loc.gov/2019980391

Contents

SECTION V: ROOTING IN LITURGY, MORAL VISION, AND VOCATION

SECTION VI: UPROOTED, REPLANTED, AND RISING

SECTION VII: GRIEF, LOVE, AND TREES

Acknowledgments

Friendship is not only one of the themes of this book—it is also the context out of which this book emerged. When the project began, its two editors had never met; even now, as the book goes to press, we have yet to meet in person. But a shared passion for God, good writing, and Earth-care (along with a shared capacity for working hard and meeting deadlines) turns out to be an excellent starting point for friendship. We both marvel at the ease with which we exchanged feedback, suggested and amended ideas, and worked together to produce and polish the writing in these pages. It was a pleasure and a blessing to collaborate on creating this anthology.

New friends were made, and existing friendships deepened and confirmed, as we gathered essays from nineteen other individuals. We are grateful to each person whose voice and witness is included in this volume: your chapters informed, moved, and inspired us. We will be drawing on the wisdom and spiritual guidance in these pages for years to come.

Thank you, Mary Evelyn Tucker and Bill McKibben for providing (respectively) a foreword and a special introduction. With eloquence and fervor, you have each spoken to the urgency of our Earth and human crisis, as well as the need for people of faith to rise to this challenge by drawing from our deepest theological, historical, liturgical, and spiritual resources. We also extend thanks to the people who suggested or helped us to contact contributors: Jim Antal, Kelly Brown Douglas, Erik Hoffner, and Peterson Toscano.

MARGARET'S WORDS OF THANKS

I would like to thank climate champion Doug Fisher (Bishop, Episcopal Diocese of Western Massachusetts) for creating the position of Missioner for Creation Care in 2014, a role that quickly went ecumenical, so that now I also serve the Massachusetts Conference, United Church of Christ. Thank you, Doug, for giving me time to develop this book and freedom to explore how my ministry can be most effective. A bow of thanks goes to my friend Jim Antal, recently Conference Minister and President of the Massachusetts Conference, UCC, and thus, for a while, my "other boss." We met, as climate activists often do, on a march (the 2007 Interfaith Walk for Climate Rescue), and have exchanged moral support ever since. It is through Jim that Leah and I first crossed paths. I am humbled and inspired by the many dedicated people who have thrown themselves into the struggle to preserve a habitable planet. Thank you, Bill McKibben, for your friendship and for leading the way.

I particularly thank Andrea Ayvazian, Marcia Black, and Kate Stevens for countless conversations, as well as my friends in Better Future Project, 350Mass for a Better Future, Climate Action Now of Western Massachusetts, National Religious Coalition on Creation Care, and Society of St. John the Evangelist. I give thanks for Bishop Bud Cederholm, for all the clergy and lay leaders I've met whose passion for climate justice and Creation care resonates with my own, and for all the people who have welcomed my itinerant ministry as preacher, teacher, and leader of spiritual retreats: your companionship means the world to me. The Empty Bell, the contemplative sanctuary that my husband founded and guides, has become a spiritual home: thank you, friends. It is a blessing to pray in silence with you and to talk with you about the ways of God. I give thanks for my mother, Sarah Doering, who entered hospice care and eventually died while this book was taking shape: your encouragement has been a light on my path. I am blessed in countless ways by my son, Sam, and by my stepdaughter Chris Labich, son-in-law Bill Labich, and grandchildren, Grace and Noah. My husband, Robert Jonas, is my soul mate, first reader, and best friend. I cherish you all.

LEAH'S WORDS OF THANKS

My father, Carl Jacobs—a landscaper, nurseryman, and conservationist—is the one who took me into the woods and taught me reverence for trees and all that lives within their ecosystems. My mother, Peggy Jacobs, filled our home with animals of all kinds—dogs, guinea pigs, rabbits, cats, birds, and, yes, humans—and taught me appreciation for nurturing life from the birth pangs to the death pains. Her parents, Thomas and Dorothy Gheen, formed some of my earliest memories of cherishing gardens, flowers, green grass, and autumn leaves. Now my husband Jim and I are cultivating this same love of greenery, animals, ecosystems, and humans within our children, Rachel and Benjamin. I am grateful for this inner circle of family who sustain me in this work.

The Pennsylvania congregations I have served—Reformation Lutheran in Media, Spirit and Truth Worship Center in Yeadon, and United in Christ Lutheran in Lewisburg—each provided a unique context within which to preach and teach about God's Creation. The environmental activists who have educated, partnered, protested, lamented, and rejoiced with me are far too numerous to list, and I am grateful for each of you. I'll mention just a few who have been key players in my own advocacy, teaching, and activism—Joy Bergey, Tracey DePasquale, Amy Reumann, Barb Jarmoska, Wendy Lynn Lee, Tink Tinker, Mordechai Liebling, Stephanie Lewis, Cynthia Moe-Lobeda, David Young, Pete Mackey, David Jacobsen, Dave and Sue Laidacker, Dale Lature, Tim Darst, Carole Devine, Scott Hardin-Nieri, Emily Askew, and Wilson Dickinson.

I am also grateful to the many organizations and groups that have been incubators of my ecological ministry: Interfaith Power & Light, Shale Justice, the Tire Burner Team and Organizations United for the Environment in central Pennsylvania, Susquehanna Valley Progressives, Green Chalice, ELCA Advocacy, Lutheran Advocacy Ministry in Pennsylvania, Lutherans Restoring Creation, Isaiah 1:17 Justice Team of the ELCA Indiana-Kentucky Synod, the Poor People's Campaign, Kentucky Council of Churches, Green Seminaries Initiative, Blessed Tomorrow and ecoAmerica, and the Green Task Force at Lexington Theological Seminary.

FINALLY

We are thankful to Rolf Janke and to Rowman & Littlefield for accepting *Rooted and Rising* for publication, and to Courtney Packard for her skillful editorial assistance. We are likewise indebted to the "peer reviewers" who studied our book proposal and not only recommended that the book be published, but also made thoughtful suggestions about its message and structure: your ideas helped to guide our thinking as we organized the final text. We are thankful for all the staff at Rowman & Littlefield who worked to place this book in readers' hands.

We dedicate this book to those who come after us. We hope that you will see that there were many of us who recognized the wrongs we had done to our Earth and took courageous steps to set things right. Where we fell short, missed the mark, or simply failed, may the legacy of love and compassion remain the longest memory.

Foreword

It is an honor to write a foreword for this inspiring collection of essays representing a wide variety of denominations and perspectives from religious traditions. It is precisely what is needed just now—namely, a call to renewed commitment for climate justice in a time of climate emergency. Each of the chapters brings us moving stories of personal struggles to speak out for climate justice against great odds. Invariably all of these religious leaders or spokespersons have found their way to the issue of the climate crisis through the lens of compassion for those who are most vulnerable and through a deep love of the Earth.

The engaging stories recounted in this book raise telling questions: Is climate change not a moral challenge? If it is, where are the widespread responses from religious communities to speak for the Earth? And if we know that the poor and vulnerable will suffer most from the effects of climate change, where are the religious voices to speak for justice?

The life stories of these authors are leading the response to these questions. And there is more. As this book makes clear, a tsunami of sadness is engulfing us and we need rituals and action to transform our grief into meaning, our sorrow into solace, our loss into hope. Where are the programs and people who will process the mourning at this time of unraveling of ecosystems and social systems in the face of hurricanes, floods, droughts, and wildfires? They are here within the pages of this book and evident in these lives that have braved the suffering to bring back a vision of transformative action. Now we ask, who will join them?

Two interrelated questions arise: Where do we begin and what can we build on? For each part of the world the response will be different, as ethics are based in different cultural, philosophical, and religious worldviews. For the United States, the task is far from easy. Although this message may be dismissed or ignored, the hard truth is that our hyperinflated lifestyle—our massive consumption of energy and goods—is contributing to the climate crisis and having adverse effects on people and the planet, both at home and abroad. With only 4 percent of the world's population, the United States consumes 25 percent of the world's resources. Moral awakening, while still elusive, is critical, and this book highlights the enormous challenges we are facing.

Yet I would suggest there are two additional strategies we can bring to the table to make a difference and turn the tide on climate change denial. One is to make more publicly known the concerns of the insurance industry regarding the reality of climate change as it impinges on affordable insurance policies. The other is to convey the concerns of the military regarding the impact of climate change on national defense. The reinsurance companies, such as Swiss RE and Munich RE, have been speaking for many years about the risks of climate change. Now primary insurance companies such as Chubb are acknowledging that human-caused climate change is real and intensifying. In April 2019, Chubb's CEO Evan Greenburg noted in his report to stockholders that the company is facing difficulties in insuring areas that are prone to fires, floods, or sea level rise. With the increased intensity and destructiveness of hurricanes such as Katrina, Sandy, and Maria, insurance companies are realizing they can no longer pay the billion-dollar costs. The experience of insurance companies should be a warning to people trying to get insurance in risky areas, such as coastal water properties. Moreover, it should serve as a wake-up call to other industries that have yet to recognize that climate change will affect every aspect of their business.

In a similar way, the U.S. Department of Defense has published several reports, the most recent one in January 2019, recognizing climate change as an issue of national security. All the U.S. naval bases stateside and abroad are at risk because of rising seas. The largest naval base in the world, in Norfolk, Virginia, is already facing continual flooding that threatens the shipbuilding yard. Constructing levees or floodgates are only temporary solutions and extremely expensive. These government-sponsored reports should encourage everyone to go beyond climate denial and move into action. Religious communities can strengthen their call for climate action by referencing these reports from the insurance industry and from the Department of Defense.

However, beyond the strategies of broadening stakeholder engagement and multiplying the courageous responses exemplified in this book lies a deeply troubling question. Does humanity have the capacity to bring forth an environmental ethic that is broad enough and inclusive enough to respond to "the cry of the Earth and the cry of the poor"?[1] The problem is that until recently, the world's mainstream religions have focused their ethical concerns primarily on human-divine relations and human-human relations and have largely ignored human-Earth relations. Failing to value nature has led to an ethical, moral, and religious vacuum. This void has thus far prevented us from developing robust environmental ethics and hindered our capacity to respond to the climate emergency.

It is largely the case at present that our religious traditions, apart from those within Native American communities, have overlooked the intrinsic value of nature and have succumbed inadvertently to a utilitarian mentality. The logic is this: "Let's use nature for humans, drilling for oil and fracking for gas, despite the consequences for both people and the planet. What's the problem with that?" Well, everything. Because the ruthless exploitation of the natural world for our own ends is undermining the health and well-being of both people and the planet.

This utilitarian mentality is being challenged by theologians such as Willie Jennings at Yale Divinity School, who is articulating a compelling Doctrine of Creation that deeply values the natural world. An ecotheological awakening has been emerging for the last several decades through the voices of process theologians such as John Cobb and Catherine Keller, ecofeminist theologians such as Rosemary Ruether and Sallie McFague, womanist theologians such as Melanie Harris, and liberation theologians such as Leonardo Boff and Ivone Gebara. Other early spokespersons were Arthur Green in the Jewish world and Seyyed Hossein Nasr in the Muslim world. The Harvard conferences on world religions and ecology in the 1990s opened up the space for all the religious traditions to move into their ecological phase. The invitation was to develop a new field in academia and a new force of religious grassroots environmentalism. This book represents the robust fruits of that movement in diverse and passionate voices working for change in synagogues, churches, and mosques.

These voices are crucial and their leadership role is indispensable for this Great Work. For it may be the case that—as with the abolitionist movement in the nineteenth century and the civil rights movement in the twentieth century—we will not respond at the scale and speed required until we see climate disruption as a moral issue and a spiritual challenge. The integration of the ethical issues of ecological degradation and climate justice into social consciousness, political legislation, and international negotiations remains to be realized. This book makes a strong contribution in that direction.

—Mary Evelyn Tucker, Yale Forum on Religion and Ecology

NOTE

1. Leonard Boff, *Cry of the Earth, Cry of the Poor* (Maryknoll, NY: Orbis Books, 1997).

A Special Introduction
by Bill McKibben

What a remarkable collection of *people* this book contains! I have been to jail with some and visited others in jail. I have joined in when some sang and marveled when some preached. I have read and learned from them all.

I remember a time when very, very few people of faith took environmental issues seriously: the topic seemed either vaguely pagan or distinctly a luxury—something to get to once war and hunger had been dealt with. And I watched with great admiration as that began to change—as Mary Evelyn Tucker and John Grim convened the remarkable gatherings that began tracing the scriptural roots of ecological concern in every major faith, and as the other leaders collected here began climbing the tree that grew from those roots.

Now that spring has turned to full summer, and that tree has leafed out in its full glory. And just in time. Because we've never needed a profound moral witness so badly. Our planet teeters on the edge. Creation is more vulnerable than ever in human history. Scientists reported in early 2019 that we'd lost half the animals that were alive on this planet in 1970—not half the species, half the *animals.* Soon after, other researchers predicted we could lose a million species by mid-century as the planet warms. As I write these words, a crushing heat wave grips India. In mid-June 2019, in the state of Bihar, government officials warned the hundred million residents not to go outdoors. Two years ago, as a warming climate spread mosquitoes that in turn spread the Zika virus, health authorities in three countries told women not to become pregnant. Think about that: not to go outdoors. Not to reproduce. The climate crisis is no longer a series of warnings; it's now a series of bulletins from the front. It is, to put it one way, getting very biblical out there.

And yet inertia retains its hold on our planet: the amount of carbon dioxide pouring into the atmosphere continues to rise each year and the temperature keeps rising. We see the sparks of what a Christian might call the Holy Spirit in action: Greta Thunberg and the school strikers; the young people with their Green New Deal; even the solar engineers making real the promise of power from heaven instead of hell. But we still need to make it count—to scale it fast enough to catch up with the ultimate opponent in this fight, which is physics. In the way stand the usual smaller obstacles: greed, sloth, the envy exploited by authoritarians. For them the only cure, finally, is love.

And love, I would suggest, is what finally roots this volume: a love for the world around us, in all its improbable glory, and for the people who alone can bear witness to that glory and rise to its defense. If they are indeed summoned to that calling, it may be in part by fear—by the proper functioning of the survival instinct. But I suspect it will be more by love, the ever-great mystery. This volume opens some windows on that mystery, because the people whose words are collected in it have been powered by that force. May they transplant it into everyone who takes this book in hand!

—Bill McKibben is the author of *Falter: Has the
Human Game Begun to Play Itself Out?* and is a founder of
350.org—the first planetwide grassroots climate change movement.

Introduction

Rev. Dr. Leah D. Schade and
Rev. Dr. Margaret Bullitt-Jonas, editors

Out of the ground the Lord God made to grow every tree that is pleasant to the sight and good for food, the tree of life also in the midst of the garden, and the tree of the knowledge of good and evil.

—Genesis 2:9

Then the angel showed me the river of the water of life, bright as crystal, flowing from the throne of God and of the Lamb through the middle of the street of the city. On either side of the river is the tree of life with its twelve kinds of fruit, producing its fruit each month; and the leaves of the tree are for the healing of the nations.

—Revelation 22:1–2

A good word is as a good tree, its root set firm and its branches in heaven, giving its fruit at every season by the leave of its Lord.

—Qur'an XIV: 24–25b

We chose the title *Rooted and Rising* for this book about climate disruption because of the universal symbolism of the tree. Nearly every religion uses the image of the tree to convey the mysterious linkage between sky and earth, the realm of the divine and the realm of humanity. The tree embodies the mysterious interchange of birth, growth, death, and new life; of soil, water, air, and sunlight; of reaching into the depths while also rising toward the heights. As we witness the ongoing and accelerating degradation of the planetary life systems that support trees—along with monarch butterflies, spade-footed toads, dolphins, human beings, and all other life-forms—these great woody plants suggest what we need to do in this perilous time. *Homo religiosus* must reach deep into our soil of scriptural and spiritual wisdom in order to draw up the life-giving water and nutrients that can sustain the trunk, branches, and leaves of the whole "family tree" that makes its home on Earth.

In the origin story of the Abrahamic faiths, human beings faced a choice that was symbolized by the tree of knowledge and made a decision that forever shaped their future with each other, with God, and with the natural world. Today humanity confronts a similar life-and-death decision. Will we choose the self-restraint that allows life to flourish, or will we grab everything for ourselves and thus sentence ourselves and other creatures to planetary collapse?

God created our brains with a prefrontal cortex that, unlike the brain of other mammals, gives us the capacity to know right from wrong and the ability to make deliberate decisions. We are at liberty to choose things that are not good and to make decisions that are self-serving. What's more, even with the best of intentions, our choices can result in unintended consequences. Over the past two hundred years, the tragic consequences of human decisions and wayward actions have been writ large. Humanity has gorged on the fruit of the tree of knowledge and has driven the Garden of Earth into ruin. The climate crisis now scorching the Earth is killing not only trees, but also glaciers, entire species of flora and fauna, and humans themselves.

Of course, this was not what we intended when we unlocked the power of fossil fuels.

The damage caused by burning coal, gas, and oil was initially innocent and inadvertent: who knew, at first, that digging up and burning long-buried carbon could possibly disrupt the global climate? Entire industries, economies, and ways of life were (and continue to be) based on energy derived from fossil fuels, and the average person thought nothing of it. However, scientists began to point out, with increasing alarm, that we had set ourselves on an increasingly deadly course. Despite the growing outcry from the scientific community, the people whose industries had caused and were profiting from this crisis denied not only their culpability, but even the fact that a crisis was occurring. They spent billions of dollars confusing and misleading the public in an ongoing effort to continue reaping profits at the expense of a livable planet. The intent was to delay as long as possible humanity's moment of moral reckoning.

The American public's widespread denial of climate change has had a stunning run. This is understandable, given that most people want to avoid thinking about something as deeply troubling as the Earth's climate crisis spiraling out of control. We humans seem to have a built-in knack for delaying as long as possible the recognition of particularly troublesome facts. Some of us even turn avoidance and denial into a fine art. As comedian George Carlin observed, "I don't believe there's any problem in this country, no matter how tough it is, that Americans, when they roll up their sleeves, can't completely ignore."

Ignore, deny, minimize—for a while we can distract ourselves from acknowledging the signs of startling disruption all around us. But the crises are now too widespread to ignore. Wildfires, propelled by drought, torch vast swathes of forests and towns. Oceans are no longer contained by shorelines but rear up to flood subway systems and wash away roads and homes. Monster hurricanes pummel us. Sweltering temperatures overheat us. Once-orderly seasons become weirdly unpredictable. The songbirds, once plentiful at our feeders, go missing.

For a while we may say to ourselves, *Things aren't that bad. The scientists are exaggerating.* Or, *This isn't my problem. I have other things to worry about.* Or, *If I don't pay attention, it will go away.* But eventually our efforts to refute the reality of a rapidly changing climate can't help but fall apart. Quickly or slowly, gradually or abruptly, there comes a time when pushing away awareness becomes impossible. Our defenses crumble. And we experience what journalist Mark Hertsgaard calls the "Oh shit" moment we all must have.[1] It's the moment when the fruit from the tree of knowledge falls from our hands, our eyes are opened, and we realize what we—and a society based on extracting fossil fuels—have done.

MARGARET'S MOMENT

I remember exactly where I was when I had my "Oh shit" moment. In the summer of 2002, I was on Thompson Island in Boston Harbor for an intensive weekend conference about the science and politics of climate change. For two and a half days we ate, drank, slept, and talked climate change. I had been concerned about global warming since 1988, when I read newspaper accounts of NASA climate scientist James Hanson's startling testimony to the U.S. Senate about the "greenhouse effect." By 2002 I'd been a climate activist for a while, so I knew most of the basics. I knew that the delicate balance of gasses in the atmosphere was shifting because of the burning of coal, gas, and oil. I knew that the scientific debate was over, and that climate change was real. I knew that we had just a short time in which to act quickly before the planet tumbled into runaway effects that would be irreversible—and catastrophic to life as we know it. I knew all this intellectually. And I was pleased with myself: I had done my homework before the workshop began. But there is a lot that a person can know intellectually without really taking it in.

As the hours went by, I took copious notes. I learned that a difference of just ten degrees can determine whether or not a planet is habitable; that we are carrying out an uncontrolled experiment on the planet's climate control system; that we are living in an increasingly narrow margin of stability. Ross Gelbspan, the Pulitzer Prize–winning newspaper editor and investigative reporter, commented that the pleasantly balmy day we'd experienced the preceding December, when Boston's temperature reached 71 degrees, was "gift wrapping on a time bomb."

Time bomb, I wrote dutifully in my notes. Keep those facts jingling like coins in a pocket. Pile them up. Bring them on. Don't feel a thing—just keep writing stuff down.

Which I did, filling up the pages with more facts about the consequences of unchecked climate change: weather-related disasters, food and water shortages, millions of refugees on the move, eruption of regional and national conflicts over increasingly scarce resources, rising seas and heating oceans, the spread of malaria and other tropical diseases, an increase in both terrorism and totalitarianism. And so on.

I did my best to stay cool and on top of the facts, but by the end of the second day, my mind was reeling, and my heart was breaking. Before bed I went outside and stood alone under the stars, trying to catch my breath, trying to assimilate what I had heard and to stop the world from tilting. Everything I loved, every aspect of the world into which I was born, was in peril. It was too much to take in, too much to handle. I was numb with shock and grief.

Oh shit.

The next morning, I grabbed my breakfast tray and went looking for the scientist who had spoken to us the night before. I told him how stunned I was by what he had told us. "How do you bear it?" I asked him. "What do you do with your feelings?"

"I don't get into my feelings," he told me. "I focus on what I can do."

I understood what he was saying. Taking action is surely an essential way to respond to the "Oh shit" moment. Labor organizer Joe Hill reportedly said from his deathbed, "Don't mourn. Organize." In a time of crisis, we need wise and levelheaded leaders who can say, "This is what we must do. Let's do it."

Yet action by itself is insufficient. Action alone won't help us integrate our grief about the unimaginable losses we face, won't help us clarify our moral outrage, won't give us strength to keep going when we suspect that our actions could fall short, come too late, and be too small to make a difference. Upon what emotional and spiritual resources do we draw when we feel overwhelmed, when our energy is flagging, when the path ahead is blocked, and we are surrounded by darkness? Once we dare to reckon with the potential collapse of the web of life and the possibility in the near future of a world that is difficult for humans to inhabit, where do we turn for meaning, purpose, and hope? What comes after the "Oh shit" moment?

LEAH'S MOMENT

My "Oh shit" moment was not a single instant of shattering insight. Rather, it has been a series of accumulating perceptions that have alternately devastated and energized me. The first of those perceptions came nearly forty years ago, although I did not recognize it at the time. It was a child's science fiction/fantasy book called *Dar Tellum: Stranger from a Distant Planet,* by James R. Berry.[2] Written in 1973, the book tells the story of a boy who, with the help of a mysterious being who communicates with him from across the universe, helps save the planet from global warming. Of course, that's not the term used at the time the book was written. It was only described as a "big crisis." When I read the story as a fifth grader in the early 1980s, I had no idea that the book would be so prescient. While it filled me with dread, it also instilled in me a sense of resolve that even a young person could help fix such a huge planetary problem.

A few years later, my sense of resolve was challenged as I witnessed the clear-cutting of two tracts of forests that were dear to me as a child. One was near my house—a wooded area where my friends and I would gather to play, gather all manner of found materials to build forts, and simply daydream under the trees' sheltering green canopy. In a single day, the bulldozers razed the trees and leveled the landscape to make room for student housing for the growing college campus. Another was a forested area in Pennsylvania where my father and I used to go hunting. We came upon a scene that looked as if a bomb had exploded. The roots of trees had been ripped from the ground and the carcasses of oak, maple, and pine were laid out for "harvesting." In both "Oh shit" moments I was crushed by the heartlessness of these acts of clear-cutting. Just as searing was the realization of how little power I had in the face of economic forces that cared nothing for the squirrels, birds, turkey, deer, and children who had called these places "home." But this realization eventually led me to study ecofeminist theology in order to understand—and resist—the patriarchal forces that are hell-bent on destroying forests, oceans, and the very atmosphere of our planet.

Since then, the "Oh shit" moments have been hitting me with increasing frequency and impact. I watched hope for a president to address climate change dangle like a "hanging chad" in the 2000 election, and then saw it flutter away with the ascension of oil-man George W. Bush. I scanned the charts of climate scientists showing the inexorable climb of carbon dioxide and methane in the atmosphere causing a feedback loop of warming, Arctic ice thawing, sea level rise, and voluminous increases in heat-trapping methane. I saw graphs of our human population exploding and consuming Earth's resources. I touched yellow flowers blooming on a forsythia bush in central

Pennsylvania at the prompting of spring-like temperatures . . . in the middle of December.

With every "Oh shit" moment and every passing year, my questions became more urgent.

Why are we doing this to ourselves? How can we stop this? How can I pastor, preach, and parent in the midst of what I call the "dark night of the green soul"? Who can I find to join me in this struggle so that our efforts for the good are multiplied and I don't feel so alone in this work?

FIGHTING THE GOOD FIGHT

Both of us have been wrestling with these questions for many years. We have thrown ourselves into activist efforts, seeking to "fight the good fight" protecting communities, waterways, land, and the very air we breathe from the ravages of the fossil fuel industry. Margaret was one of the first faith leaders to engage in civil disobedience to protest policies that lead to global warming. In 2001 she was arrested with twenty-one other people at the U.S. Department of Energy in Washington, D.C., during an interfaith prayer vigil to oppose oil drilling in the Arctic National Wildlife Refuge. Since then she has risked arrest multiple times, lobbied, and marched; spoken at climate rallies, conferences, and energy hearings; led public prayers, fasted in front of the White House, and worked with an activist network to push the Episcopal Church to divest from fossil fuels (a decision the Church made in 2015). Margaret left parish ministry in 2013 to give her full attention to mobilizing communities of faith to respond to climate change. She is now Missioner for Creation Care in the Episcopal Diocese of Western Massachusetts and the United Church of Christ in Massachusetts.

Leah was at the forefront of the anti-fracking movement in Pennsylvania, helping to lead protests and advocate for vulnerable communities. She has testified at EPA hearings and worked with interfaith groups to address climate change. In 2012, she was the primary faith leader involved in the "Save Riverdale" campaign. In Williamsport, Pennsylvania, hundreds of people from across the country gathered to help a low-income, mobile home community along the Susquehanna River that was slated for destruction in order to make way for a water withdrawal plant for the fracking industry. In the end, the economic and political forces arrayed against the activists—and backed by the police—had their way, but the effort drew national attention to the predatory, destructive nature of the fracking industry and its related businesses. Also, from 2012 to 2014, Leah worked as a community organizer to stop a proposed tire incinerator that threatened the air quality of her rural Pennsylvania region. In a campaign that touched nearly every public sector and involved hundreds of volunteers, the burner was eventually defeated, and the community was spared.

Both of us have spent years carrying out our work with the conviction that it was essential to make connections across political, religious, racial/ethnic, and socioeconomic divides. Both of us have drawn from our religious faith and dared to hope that, even though our federal government's response to the climate crisis was agonizingly slow; even though the fossil fuel industry remained bent on extracting and burning additional coal, gas, and oil; and even though the American public had not yet grasped the urgency of the hour, human beings could nevertheless succeed in bringing back our planet from the brink of catastrophic climate change.

THEN 2016 HAPPENED

With the election of Donald Trump and control of all three branches of government passing into the hands of the Republican Party, those of us concerned about the web of life and the future of the human enterprise realized with a shock that our national government was no longer going to be frustratingly slow in addressing the unprecedented crises of climate change and species extinction. It was now going to form an unabashed and robust alliance with the fossil fuel industry to charge ahead with fossil fuels rather than embrace alternative forms of energy. Among the president's first acts was the appointment of Rex Tillerson as secretary of state, the chairman and chief executive officer of the world's largest oil and gas corporation. Our national government was also now going to rapidly and deliberately dismantle whatever regulations and policies were in place to protect clean air, clean water, public health, a stable climate, and a habitable planet. The Keystone XL pipeline was quickly approved. The Standing Rock encampment was disbanded as President Trump authorized the pipeline that would desecrate Native lands and threaten the tribal water supply. U.S. partnership in the worldwide effort to address climate change collapsed when Trump announced that our country would withdraw from the Paris Climate Accord.

Meanwhile, the head of the Environmental Protection Agency, Scott Pruitt, quickly set about repealing, delaying, or blocking countless regulations aimed at mitigating climate change, including the Clean Power Plan. Ryan Zinke, Secretary of the Interior, handed nearly two million acres of the Bears Ears and Grand Staircase-Escalante National Monuments to developers, loggers, and fossil fuel companies, and opened up previously protected federal lands for drilling and mining. Drilling in the Arctic National Wildlife Refuge was now back on the table, as was opening up new offshore oil and gas drilling in nearly all U.S. coastal waters.

All of this was happening while global atmospheric levels of carbon dioxide reached more than 400 parts per million (ppm) for the first time since record-keeping began. This is far above the 350-ppm threshold generally considered the safe upper limit for avoiding catastrophic climate change. In 2017, a series of devastating hurricanes propelled by climate change pummeled the Gulf Coast, tore across the Caribbean and up through Florida, and created a humanitarian crisis in Puerto Rico and the U.S. Virgin Islands. Wildfires, accelerated by high winds, extreme heat, and bone-dry landscapes, destroyed more than one million acres of land across California. Then the rains fell, creating lethal mudslides and flooding.

Elsewhere, droughts ravaged Kenya and Somalia. Floods, monsoons, and landslides wiped out millions of homes and killed hundreds of people in countries that included India, Bangladesh, Nepal, Sri Lanka, Zimbabwe, Sierra Leone, China, Peru, and Columbia. These were just the kinds of extreme weather events that scientists had warned would result from unmitigated climate change.

As we write this, fast-melting glaciers in Antarctica continue to break off into the sea as ocean levels rise along coastlands, flood communities, and swallow island nations. Coral reefs worldwide are bleaching and dying. Billions of populations of plants, fish, and animals have been lost in recent decades in what scientists are calling a "biological annihilation." We are in the midst of the sixth mass extinction event since life began on this planet. Because of warming seas, the level of oxygen in the ocean is rapidly dropping; in the open ocean, dead zones with zero oxygen have quadrupled in size since 1950. The ocean is beginning to suffocate. All these drastic changes provoke or intensify human suffering and particularly harm the poor, communities of color, women, and children. We are driving ourselves into an ecological "East of Eden."

Scientific reports have become increasingly dire. A late-2018 special report from the United Nations' scientific advisory board, the Intergovernmental Panel on Climate Change (IPCC), contends in the starkest possible terms that only a transformation of human social and economic systems—historically unprecedented in both scope and speed—can avert climate chaos. Nevertheless, the federal government under the Trump regime remains staunchly on the side of the polluters, relentlessly pushing ahead with decisions that change federal policy to make it easier for companies to pollute. At the time of this writing, both the EPA and the Interior Department are headed by former fossil fuel industry lobbyists—indeed, the whole administration is filled with former corporate lobbyists.

Of course, there is good news, too, such as rapid technological advances, a steep drop in the cost of solar energy, and widespread pushback to the energy and environmental policies of the current administration across a wide spectrum of American businesses, municipalities, and organizations. After the mid-term election, one-party rule in Washington, D.C., came to an end in 2019 as Democrats took their seats in the House, bringing with them a fresh commitment to climate action and a range of bold new policies under the umbrella term Green New Deal. The global, grassroots climate movement is growing. More than one thousand institutions around the world have committed to divesting from fossil fuels. Inspired by the Swedish climate activist Greta Thunberg—a teenager—hundreds of thousands of students around the world have started walking out of classes, determined to hold their governments to account for climate inaction. Anti-pipeline protests, many of them led by indigenous peoples, are being carried out worldwide. As you will see in these pages, people of faith with incredible stamina and unrelenting courage are mobilizing worldwide to preserve what is left of our planet. We know that this movement will continue to build in strength and numbers in the years ahead.

Still, the hour is late, the stakes are high, the obstacles are great, and the time left for effective action is terrifyingly short. It's no wonder that many people are slipping into despair. When reputable scientists are debating the timeline for reaching Earth's capacity to sustain human life—do we have three hundred years left? fifty? maybe ten?—the existential crisis becomes immediate and crushing.

LAMENT, RESILIENCE, AND ACTION

As the two of us have grappled with this reality, we felt it imperative that this volume express sorrow and despair with the honesty of biblical lament. Like the angel in the Book of Revelation, we want to proclaim with a loud voice, "Do not damage the earth or the sea or the trees" (Revelation 7:3). Like the prophet Hosea, we grieve that "there is . . . no knowledge of God in the land. . . . Therefore the land mourns, and all who live in it languish; together with the wild animals and the birds of the air, even the fish of the sea are perishing" (Hosea 4:1b, 3). Lament is a manifestation of the human spirit that can break through apathy and numbness, creating a space for hope and action.

Yet lamentation is not enough. We are parents of children and we are leaders within our respective faith communities whose members look to us for a way forward. We are clergy whose congregations have turned to us for an authentic word of hope. We have friends and colleagues who have linked arms with us to face the future with courage. And we worship a God who, in the Christian tradition, promises resurrection, even after all hope has been crucified.

More strongly than ever, we appreciate the deep need for spiritual resilience in the face of massive upheaval. We also believe that the climate crisis can become a doorway to a new way of inhabiting Earth. The emergency in which we find ourselves can serve as a catalyst for spiritual and societal transformation. It is our deepest, most fervent hope that the wisdom of the world's religious and faith traditions can help to midwife whatever new life will be born out of this cataclysmic time.

So we challenged our colleagues in the faith-and-climate movement to join us in sharing their stories of struggle and strength and to give us a glimpse of what sustains them when they are frustrated, depressed, or despondent. We wanted to hear about their sources of hope and to learn what keeps them going in the struggle for a just and sustainable future. These writers represent a wide range of faiths, ages, genders/sexualities, cultures, and contexts. They come from across the spectrum of leadership, scholarship, and activism, and from diverse social, cultural, ethnoracial, and religious locations.

Our authors include faith leaders, community organizers, scientists, theologians, and grassroots climate activists. Some of them are well-known public figures; others are people whose commitment to climate justice is known mostly to their local community. All of them are united around the scriptural "Tree of Life" in dedicating their energy and vision to finding solutions to the climate crisis and to serving the common good, even when the challenges are daunting and the success of their efforts is uncertain.

We offer this book to everyone who is seeking spiritual meaning and strength as they take action to stabilize the climate and to build a more equitable society. And we dedicate these essays to future generations, to the people struggling to make a life in a harsher, hotter, more turbulent planet than the one into which we were born. We hope that the stories, vision, resolve, and practices that are found in these pages will be of use not only to those who are alive today but perhaps also to those who come after us. This is not a book about facts and figures, charts and numbers. This is a book about personal stories and testimony, about witnessing to what we love, what we yearn for, what we mourn, and what we are fiercely committed to protecting.

As you read through the essays, you will notice that, with their own distinctive voices, the authors draw from the depths of their faith and help us rise to meet the challenges we face. Some of them share a story about losing and finding hope. Others share spiritual practices or perspectives that help them to stay grounded and to cultivate a peaceful heart. Each of them reveals the spiritual roots of their activism that enable them to rise each day and keep going.

All the contributors either spring from or have deep connections with the Abrahamic faiths—even when those connections are contested or challenged. What we all share are common core values of caring about the natural world, social justice, inclusion, and interfaith hospitality. We understand that justice movements are interlinked—that the fight for climate justice is intimately tied to the fight for racial, gender, and economic justice. Climate change intersects with—and exacerbates—nearly every other justice issue, from hunger to homelessness, from refugees to racism. Thus, each of the writers represents a nexus of these interrelated issues. Even if you don't identify with a particular religious tradition, we believe that these writers have something to say to anyone who is seeking wisdom, strength, and hope in the face of an uncertain future. We trust that the depth and honesty of these essays will refresh you.

In all humility, we recognize, as Lynn White argued in his now famous 1967 essay "The Historical Roots of Our Ecologic Crisis," that the Judeo-Christian tradition bears a burden of responsibility for creating theologies that have treated the natural world as merely a backdrop for the drama of human salvation.[3] Or, even worse, nature has been regarded as only a throwaway set piece to be used and destroyed. Even today, politicians like Scott Pruitt cite the Bible and employ a distorted interpretive lens of exploitation when they promote policies that harm the Earth. However, as White contends, it is up to the world's religions to help humanity envision a way forward that is based on life-nourishing values of love, justice, and care for God's Creation.

Especially as we mark the fiftieth anniversary of the first Earth Day, coordinated by Denis Hayes in 1970, this book invites its readers to celebrate justice-seeking, life-affirming forms of faith, spiritual practice, and action that treat Earth and all its residents—human and other-than-human—as a sacred, living whole. We hope to give our readers material for personal reflection and prayer, sermons, congregational book studies, and interfaith conversations. Above all, we hope that these essays will spark your imagination, strengthen your resolve, and encourage you to identify your own sources of spiritual resilience and resistance to be rooted and rising in a time of extraordinary planetary challenge.

Finally, this book is not about trying to convince people of the urgent need to care for the natural world. There are plenty of excellent books already written on that subject. (See the bibliography for a list of some of those resources.) Our concern here is how to move forward, given what we know: how much has been lost, how much devastation lies ahead, and how much creativity, persistence, and courage it will take to create a better future. When it comes to climate change, all of our contributors have experienced the "Oh shit" moment, yet have found a way to regain their footing, make meaning, and take the next step.

The volume is organized into seven groups of three authors. The section themes encompass interfaith friendship; local activism; science and policy; voices from the margins; liturgy, moral vision, and vocation; being uprooted; and grief, love, and trees. While themes in many of the essays overlap, we wanted to bring a particular trio of voices together in each section as dialogue partners to highlight what they share in common, as well as the ways in which their contrasting perspectives raise important insights. Each section begins with a brief introduction and concludes with a set of discussion questions and spiritual practices.

Because we hold prophetic spirituality in high regard, at the end of each section we suggest a spiritual practice that can steady our minds, open our hearts, and renew our strength as we connect with the struggle for social and ecological justice. Trusting that the Holy may be found in many places, we offer exercises and practices that resonate with or spring from a variety of faith traditions. All of them work for individual use; some can also be adapted for small-group or large-group settings and can even be used in worship services. Each of them is time-tested and has been a source of strength and resilience for one or both of this book's editors. We hope that some of these spiritual practices will become a new tool in your own array of resources.

As you read the reflections of these authors, reflect on the study questions, and explore the spiritual practices, we hope you'll agree that our present crisis can elicit a depth of wisdom, insight, and motivation that can guide us—as individuals and as a society—toward a more peaceful, just, and Earth-honoring future. We sincerely thank you for opening this book and opening yourself to that which is Sacred and Holy. May you be blessed with the gifts of listening and learning, prayer and ritual, resilience and community, contemplation and action.

Editor's note: We capitalize the word "Creation" throughout the book so as to denote the level of respect we afford the world as subject rather than object. We do the same with the term "Earth" when addressing it as an entity (as opposed to lowercase earth, *a synonym of soil).*

QUESTIONS TO PONDER

1. The introduction describes some of the many ways that climate change is already disrupting life around the world. Which of these impacts most concerns you or most captures your attention? How has climate change affected your town or region? What changes have you noticed? What do you feel as you consider what lies ahead for your community and our planet? What most alarms you?

2. The editors describe their "Oh shit" moments when they realized the severity of climate disruption and its implications for life on this planet. They name the despair that can follow such profound realization as enter-

ing the "dark night of the green soul." How would you describe your own "Oh shit" moment or your own "dark night of the green soul"? Who or what has helped you to work it through?

3. Lament, resilience, and action are highlighted as essential responses to the climate crisis. Each of us may go through different "seasons" of emphasizing one over the others. Which of these responses has resonated most strongly for you in the past? Which of these responses is most prominent in your life right now? Which response might need more of your attention in the days ahead?

A SPIRITUAL PRACTICE

Creating a Sacred Space

People who take up a regular practice of prayer or meditation often find it helpful to create a special place in their home where they can practice without distraction. It might be a corner of your bedroom or another quiet spot where you can close the door, turn off the phone, sit in silence, and give prayer or meditation your full attention. If this accords with your tradition, you might wish to set up a simple altar with a candle, plant, or image that reminds you of your intention to create a peaceful, sacred space. If space is limited and you can't set aside a place for prayer, you might try something as simple as choosing a special cloth or candle to put beside you when it is time to pray. Establishing a beautiful setting and calm atmosphere for prayer supports our intention to slow down, notice what is going on, and seek the Holy. Creating a sacred space that is outside us can also help us to recognize and uphold the sacred space that is inside us.

NOTES

1. Mark Herstgaard, quoted by Anna Fahey, in "Fatherhood Confronts Climate Change," *Yes* Magazine, July 1, 2011, https://www.yesmagazine.org/issues/beyond -prisons/fatherhood-confronts-climate-change. This is Fahey's book review of Herstgaard's *Hot: Living through the Next Fifty Years on Earth* (Boston: Mariner Books, 2011).

2. James R. Berry, *Dar Tellum: Stranger from a Distant Planet*, illustrated by Ken Longtemps (New York: Scholastic Book Services, 1973).

3. Lynn Townsend White Jr. "The Historical Roots of Our Ecologic Crisis," *Science* 155, no. 3767 (March 10, 1967): 1203–7.

Section I

ROOTING IN
INTERFAITH FRIENDSHIP

Section I Introduction

This book is rooted in interfaith friendships. Many of the authors have known each other for years and even decades, while some friendships have been formed quite recently. These connections are like the roots of trees linking deep beneath the soil. Scientists have recently learned that trees communicate with each other through an underground fungal network that connects through their root systems. Sometimes called the "wood wide web," this complex interchange between trees allows them to share resources, alert each other about pests, and nurture seedlings. The first three chapters in this book point to these connections that reach across human divides while also honoring the rich religious traditions of the authors. All three writers—Mordechai Liebling, Huda Alkaff, and Leah D. Schade—have worked with interfaith coalitions in their climate activism while also rooting firmly in their respective faiths. Their voices set the tone for the spirit of dialogue that animates this collection.

Chapter One

Living in the Four Worlds

Spiritual Practices in the Midst of Climate Disruption

Rabbi Mordechai Liebling

"If someone had tapped David on his way to fight Goliath and asked, 'David, are you hopeful?' David would have pushed him out of the way and said, 'I've got a job to do.'" That is how my teacher Joanna Macy approaches the question of hope. Our engaging in action to fight the Corporate Goliath does not depend on our being hopeful. I follow the nearly 2,000-year-old teaching of Rabbi Tarfon: "You are not obligated to complete the work, but neither are you free to desist from it" (Pirkei Avot [Ethics of the Fathers] 2:21).

Jewish mysticism teaches that we are always living in four worlds: physical, emotional, intellectual, and spiritual. I need to be able to care for myself in each of these aspects of life in order to be able to sustain myself as an environmental activist. Here are some of the ways I connect with the Life Force of the universe, understand the world around me, open my heart, and ground my body.

It is hard to look at the facts of climate disruption, to accept that we are headed full steam ahead toward massive environmental disruption and social chaos. The truth is that the lives of my children and grandchildren are seriously threatened. What helps me to face that truth is that both of my parents were Holocaust survivors. Both of them lost their entire families; after the war they were refugees; eventually they made it to America and were able to rebuild their lives. I grew up surrounded by my parents' friends, all survivors. I experienced firsthand their amazing resiliency and love of life. I saw that people could experience unimaginable destruction and pain and still maintain their humanity with open and loving hearts.

Twice I have gone on week-long meditation retreats to Auschwitz-Birkenau with the Zen Peacemakers. Each day we sat for several hours next to the railroad tracks where the prisoners were unloaded and selected for immediate death or slave labor. The basic meditation instruction we received was,

"Auschwitz is the teacher." There was no hiding from the truth of the horrors perpetrated there. We also listened to stories from survivors. What I found extraordinary is the amount of *love* that was present in the death camps. In the face of the most brutal dehumanization imaginable, prisoners insisted on their humanity and took care of each other.

One example that I heard as a child is from Genya, a friend of my mom's, who was a teenager while in Auschwitz. While on starvation rations, she and a few friends saved some crumbs every day in order to make a "birthday cake" for another friend.

I learned that we are capable of withstanding great tragedy when we have loving relationships.

We are alive at the moment of the most rapid rate of change ever in both the natural and human-made worlds. Our neurological circuits are not accustomed to taking in this amount of information and change so quickly; this leads to feelings of uncertainty. The generation that grew up during the Cold War was the first to experience existential anxiety about humankind as a whole. While the threat of ecological or nuclear disaster may lurk in the minds of many people today, environmental activists go further: they consciously face the danger and immerse themselves in knowing the probabilities of global catastrophe. Yet, none of us knows exactly what will happen. All of us must therefore cultivate the ability to live with uncertainty while maintaining loving relationships.

I find that to live and be effective in a world of uncertainty I need to be grounded in the Earth, in myself, in my connection to others, in awareness, and in Judaism. On most mornings, for well more than forty years, I have maintained a practice of doing some form of bodywork or meditative movement for thirty to ninety minutes. As part of that, I take some time to ground myself in the Earth. I usually imagine roots coming out of the soles of my feet and intermingling with the soil, rocks, and tree roots. Sometimes, with each out-breath, I visualize my roots going deeper and deeper into the earth, then to the aquifers below, then further to the dense rock and on to the fiery core; and with each in-breath I breathe the energy of that layer up through my legs into my lower back (first chakra) and my palms. At times I visualize the energy center above my head (seventh chakra), and with each in-breath I inhale the energy of the cosmos to that point and exhale that energy down my spine to my center, just below my navel (second chakra). After a while, I breathe energy from the cosmos into the Earth and then back up again. This connects me to the heavens and the Earth.

Mindfulness meditation is another practice that helps me to stay grounded within myself and within Judaism. I was trained as a Jewish mindfulness meditation teacher. I try to go yearly to a weeklong silent retreat in a Jewish context. This practice cultivates the awareness that everything is always changing and that it is only in the present moment that we can cultivate awareness. Doing this in a Jewish context also leads me to reflect on Jewish teachings and to clarify the intellectual and theological framework within which I view the world.

I find the Buddhist practice of *metta*—loving-kindness meditation—very helpful in keeping my heart open and strengthening my connection to others. It is also one tool to keep me from dehumanizing the people whose policies and actions I oppose. There are a variety of ways of practicing *metta* that can easily be found online or learned from a Buddhist teacher. This is something you can try even now: sit in a relaxed meditative pose and repeat a set of phrases wishing yourself and others in the world well-being.

During my second meditation retreat at Auschwitz I meditated on this: What does forgiveness mean? At the end of the week I practiced *metta* meditation for the prisoners, the dead, and the guards. I find that love is a much better motivator and sustainer of activism than anger.

Naturally, I get angry when reading or hearing about yet another terrible piece of news. Anger may be a catalyst for action, but connecting with what I love is a better guide than anger will ever be for deciding which actions to take. Opening to love requires feeling our own pain. Obviously, we can't stop to feel our pain deeply every time we hear bad news, but if we numb ourselves and never feel it, our days of activism—our days of feeling alive—are numbered. As Joanna Macy teaches, "Feeling the pain is a measure of our humanity."[1] The numbing of our individual and collective consciousness is one of the greatest dangers that human beings face. I know that sometimes I need to allow myself to listen to the news and cry, because weeping keeps my heart open. But most of the time I just need to breathe into the news, be mindful of it, and then allow it to pass through me.

Finally, I also find it essential to stay connected with a community. For the past eight years I have been part of a Be the Change action/study circle. We are a group of eleven who meet a couple of times a month. Inspired by the Pachamama Alliance,[2] we begin every meeting with the following invocation:

We support each other to be the change to bring forth a more environmentally sustainable, socially just, and spiritually fulfilling human presence on this planet, our Mother Earth.

Whenever we gather we have a personal check-in, discuss the reading we assigned ourselves, and talk about the implications for action, occasionally engaging in a spiritual practice. We share what activism each of us is involved in, provide support, and frequently go to actions together. We have developed a strong sense of mutual accountability that empowers each of us to be more effective. We support one another to look at the truth of climate disruption and to respond boldly and faithfully.

Studying the issues allows us to create a political analysis of environmental injustice and destruction. To be in the work for a long time requires us to think about power and systems. We must ask, What is the system that is causing this? How is power exercised? What needs to be changed?

I have discovered that, for me, engaging in one-off actions or limited campaigns is not effective and can lead to burnout. I have learned that I need to see everything in a larger context. Our group understands that the paradigm of domination of Earth and people lies at the heart of all industrial societies and that global capitalism is the economic system that is driving the crisis. We also study how racism determines who will feel the worst impacts of the degradation of the planet. Developing this larger understanding gives us a long-term perspective on the work we are doing.

The Philadelphia synagogue to which I belong, Mishkan Shalom, provides another source of strength. Because I live in a large city, I have the good fortune to be able to belong to a synagogue that values social justice as a core commitment. It is rejuvenating to attend services where the prayers and teachings affirm that there can be no separation between justice, sustainability, and Spirit. This conviction emanates from the core teachings of Judaism.

Much of what I have learned about spiritual grounding for sacred activism came to life in 2017, when I spent nearly a week at the Standing Rock encampment. Standing Rock embodied what it looks like to act for justice and sustainability in the wake of genocide while being guided by Spirit. The Native American leadership created a strong container, a sturdy holding environment in which everything took place. They insisted that everything be done in accordance with traditional ways. Their practices showed that it was possible for a few thousand people to gather, self-organize, create community, maintain accountability, respect each other, and act powerfully in the face of militarized corporate and state power. When we entered the area where the pipeline was being built and knew that the police were going to confront us and order us to leave, we were instructed by the Elders to behave as though we were engaged in sacred ceremony. There would be no violence, no angry words or disrespect. While the battle to stop that pipeline was lost, the resistance movement centered at Standing Rock created an enduring model for sacred action. Just as "Auschwitz was the teacher," we learned that "Standing Rock is the teacher." We listened to the community and discovered once again an extraordinary amount of love in the midst of brutal inhumanity.

Increasingly, I find wisdom and support in Judaism's essential teachings about how we are to be in the world, especially this teaching from Micah 6:6: "God has told you what is good, and what does The Breath of Life require of you: Only to do justice, and to love goodness, and to walk modestly with your God." As a white, cisgendered, heterosexual man, I find the injunction to walk "modestly" particularly compelling. *Modestly* means that I understand that part of what I have achieved, part of the leadership role that I get to play, is related to the privileges that I enjoy. *Modestly* means that I understand that I must listen to other people's experiences and points of view. *Modestly* means that I need to keep my heart and my mind open. *Modestly* means that I don't always need to have the right answer or to know the right course of action, which is a relief to my superego.

All these practices encourage me to rest in the web of life, the connective tissue/energy of the universe that is God. When I imagine roots emanating from the soles of my feet into the earth, when I tap into the pain I feel in response to destruction or injustice, or when I celebrate the joy of being in loving community I know that I am not alone, but can lean into God as the Life Force.

"We don't know how we will serve YHVH until we get there," Moses said to Pharaoh (Exodus 10:26). We live in the midst of uncertainty; we can only show up in the present moment. I don't know what the "best" path of action is; I can only discern how I think I will be most effective and what my best next step should be. I don't know if we will succeed in avoiding a climate tipping point of no return. In fact, I doubt that we will. But I know that love is what makes life meaningful, and that building loving relationships and community is the path most likely to get us through catastrophes and horrific events. My primary task is to work on becoming more present and loving and to create loving community.

NOTES

1. Joanna Macy, "The Hidden Promise of Our Dark Age: Discovering Our Wisdom, Strength and Beauty in the Midst of Crisis" (speech, Bioneers Conference, San Rafael, CA, October 2009), https://www.youtube.com/watch?v=vzmjF1jE2K0. This was preceded by a long introduction by Nina Simmons, the co-founder of Bioneers.

2. As stated on its website, the Pachamama Alliance is "a global community that offers people the chance to learn, connect, engage, travel and cherish life for the purpose of creating a sustainable future that works for all." "About," Pachamama Alliance, https://www.pachamama.org/about.

Chapter Two

Connecting Faith, Environmental Justice, and Sustainability

An Islamic Reflection

Huda Alkaff

Believe it or not, I have been an environmentalist since I was a child. I remember being asked the famous question: "What do you want to be when you grow up?" To everyone's surprise, my answer was: an ecologist, an environmentalist—even though I did not know what it meant! I was and still am fascinated by nature and all its inhabitants, and I wanted to learn more about them and the connections between them.

When I was a child, we had a small garden where my parents and I planted vegetables and flowers. We had rabbits and cats, and I was in charge of taking care of the garden and the animals (with help from my parents, of course). That garden was a world of discovery and joy for me and has become a treasure of stories and memories. I celebrated rain then and now in pure Islamic spiritual appreciation of water—a sacred life-giving gift and trust. Another lovely place of childhood memories is the sea: walking barefoot on the beach; marveling over the beautiful, intricate, and colorful shells; and sharing my own stories with the curling and smiling waves. I was curious to learn about the puzzles of the garden, sea, water, shells, stars, birds, and fish. Although I loved to play with challenging jigsaw puzzles, the puzzles of the wonders of nature were more intriguing to comprehend and solve.

Joyful moments of observing the new crescent moon or the sunrise are spiritually rich and fulfilling for me. They are precious times of awe, wonder, and reflection. Sighting the new crescent always provides a fresh opportunity to celebrate the movement of the moon in its phases (new moon through full moon to new crescent) for the Islamic lunar Hijri calendar. Likewise, we follow the movement of the sun for the Islamic schedule of five daily prayers (Fajr/dawn, Dhuhr/noon, Asr/afternoon, Maghrib/sunset, and Isha'/evening prayers). Guided by prayer we can be in a continuous state of Hijra—migration from the bad to the good and toward better conditions for all humanity.

Inspired by the natural world, I earned two undergraduate degrees—in chemistry and biology—yet I yearned for a more interdisciplinary field of study. Ecology is the study of interconnections and interdependence among everything in space and time. I invested my time and energy in two higher education degrees—science/environmental education and conservation ecology, and sustainable development. Even so, the inner search for spiritual meaning continued.

It is a duty and obligation for Muslims to care for Earth, our common home. God states in the Qur'an, the Holy Book for Muslims, "It is God who has made you viceroys on earth" (6:165). The earth is mentioned more than 450 times in the Qur'an. There are approximately 1,500 environmental messages in the Qur'an and the Hadith (reports on the sayings and traditions of the Prophet Muhammad, God's peace and blessings be upon him [PBUH]) that guide Muslims toward care for all God's creatures and for sacred gifts and natural resources such as water, air, food, light, land, and so on. Some of the Qur'an's chapter titles are the following: The Cow, The Honey-Making Bees, The Light, The Ants, The Spider, The Star, The Iron, The People, The Pen, The Dawn, The Sun, The Moon, The Night, The Day, The Fig, The Elephant, and so on. There are many stories, signs (*ayyat*), and lessons related to the natural world. *Be like a Tree* and *Be like a Bee* are some of the lessons in Islamic teachings.

God mentions grapes, onions, garlic, lentils, and many other plants and fruits in the Qur'an. God states in the Qur'an,

> It is God who produceth gardens with trellises and without, and dates and tilth with produce of all kinds, and olives and pomegranates similar [in kind] and different [in variety]: eat of their fruit in their season but render the dues that are proper on the day of harvest. And be not excessive. Indeed, He does not like those who commit excess. (6:141)

In Islam, there are clear teachings and signs about the important, beautiful, and intricate balance of Creation. God repeatedly tells us to maintain that balance and not to upset the order in Creation. In the Qur'an, God says, "And the earth We have spread out; set thereon mountains firm and immovable; and produced therein all kinds of things in due balance" (15:19). He instructs us, "Eat and drink of that which God has provided (and permitted) and do not act corruptly, causing mischief on earth" (2:60). Humankind is advised to be moderate in every aspect of life, as we are taught in the Qur'an, "O Children of Adam . . . eat and drink: but waste not by excess, for God loveth not the wasters" (7:31). The Prophet Muhammad (PBUH) forbade a person to waste water even in washing for prayer on the bank of an abundantly flowing river.

At this time of darkness due to environmental and climate injustices suffered by the most vulnerable, including current and future generations in this country and around the world, it is important for us to do everything we can. The Prophet Mohammed (PBUH) is reported to have said, "If doomsday is about to take place while anyone of us has a tree sapling in our hand, which we can cultivate, then cultivate it for we will be rewarded." This message of active hope inspires me. Personally, I strive to seek the light in the midst of every dark and difficult situation, including this time of climate disruption.

One day in 2000, I was excited to hear about an interfaith environmental group in my home state of Wisconsin. I contacted them to ask when and how to join. I was shocked by their reply: "No, we do not accept Muslims." That was a painful time for me, and I feel that same sharp pain now with the rise in Islamophobia around us. During this time of darkness, it is especially important to work for light, love, unity, and climate justice, and to stand up together against hate, division, and racism. Our collective effort is to embrace each other in mutual respect, not turning our backs on those who are marginalized and vulnerable. As the Qur'an teaches, "And God has set up the Balance (of Justice), in order that ye may not transgress (due) balance. So establish weight with justice and fall not short in the balance: It is God Who has spread out the earth for all God's creatures" (55:7–10). Similarly, we read, "These are the Signs of God: We rehearse them to thee in Truth: And God means no injustice to any of God's creatures" (Qur'an 3:108).

Islamic teachings are rich with environmental messages, so the true practice of Islam means living simply, treading lightly on Earth, caring for our neighbors and all creatures, standing up for justice, and collaborating with others for the common good. People of faith, Muslims included, have a great responsibility to stand up for environmental justice and to address the concerns and calamities of poor and marginalized communities. This is especially the case regarding those with the lowest ecological footprints who are, ironically and tragically, the very people most affected by environmental and climate disasters. Different faith traditions standing united for environmental justice and care of creation are mobilizing the faithful for the common good.

After the rejection I received in 2000, I dedicated my life to building interfaith relationships and collaborations. In 2005, I founded Wisconsin Green Muslims, a statewide grassroots environmental justice volunteer group that connects faith and sustainability through education and service. It seeks to educate the Muslim community and the general public about Islamic environmental teachings, to apply these teachings in daily life, and to form coalitions with others working toward a just, healthy, peaceful, and sustainable future. The effort to uncover and establish connections and to understand the world holistically drives my ongoing work to build strong and sustainable bridges

between the environmental teachings in Islam (and other faiths and spiritualities) and my academic training in ecology.

Our work is guided and inspired by sacred teachings from the Qur'an and the
Hadith. Since 2005, Wisconsin Green Muslims has worked on environmental
justice issues related to climate change, clean air, pure water, healthy food,
solar energy and energy efficiency, waste reduction, and transportation equity.
Green Ramadan is one of our successful campaigns, during which we celebrate
the holy month of the Qur'an and daily fasting from dawn until dusk with daily
actions to reduce our ecological footprints and consumption impacts.

Currently, Wisconsin Green Muslims has two interfaith initiatives: "Wisconsin Faith and Solar" and "Faithful Rainwater Harvesting," or FaRaH,
which means *joy* in Arabic. These initiatives connect faith communities with
the unifying powers of sunlight and rainwater as sacred trusts and gifts, while
providing valuable peer learning and education, assessments, and collaborative
benefits to advance equitable solar energy and to provide solutions to flooding.

On August 18, 2015, a bold Islamic Declaration on Global Climate Change
was released. Its message resonates with the papal encyclical that was released earlier that year, *Laudato Si'—Praise Be to You: On Care for Our
Common Home*. The declaration calls for a rapid phase-out of fossil fuels and
a switch to 100 percent renewable energy, as well as increased support for
vulnerable communities and climate refugees already suffering from global
climate impacts. Similarly, I am pleased with our budding national Greening
Ramadan campaign with more than sixty Mosques participating—a number
that grows each year. Recently the largest Muslim organization in the United
States, the Islamic Society of North America, announced its decision to divest
from fossil fuels, a decision that other faith communities have made as well.

The Wisconsin Faith, Environmental Justice and Solar Initiative is an interfaith program built on the foundation of trust in the unifying power of solar
energy to bring people of faith and good will together to care for Earth, save
money to reinvest in their missions, and move forward toward an equitable,
100-percent-renewable energy future. It received high approval ratings from
people from diverse geographical, age, gender, and political backgrounds,
providing solar education, assessments, and consultations to more than 2,500
people of at least eighteen different religions and spiritualities in Wisconsin—and counting.

Both initiatives have three components. The first involves a social and
educational component consisting of a peer learning circle of those who have
built solar or green infrastructure and those aspiring to do so. The second is
the financial component, where we provide free and/or discounted remote
and on-site solar assessments and consultations. We love spreading the good
news, telling people, "This is a solar-promising site!" The third component

is spiritual. We see sunlight and water as "the commons." No one owns them, and everyone should have *responsible* access to them. Both sunlight and water are sacred gifts and sacred trusts. We need to appreciate them and welcome them with care into our homes, congregations, and lives.

We've also found that our interfaith efforts can not only heal our relationship with Earth, but also build interfaith acceptance. For example, with support from the Climate Advocacy Lab in studying the impact of the unifying power of solar in helping overcome Islamophobia in Wisconsin, we compared the differences in the framing effects of our message. We surveyed Wisconsinites on their responses to either a Muslim frame or Christian frame in our literature. Using Google consumer surveys, we presented different samples of literature with a photo of either a female Muslim wearing a hijab (which happened to be my personal photo!) or a female Christian pastor wearing a clerical collar. Both pieces included the same statement: "Solar energy reduces air pollution, saves money, and creates jobs in our communities—which is why religious groups across Wisconsin are installing solar panels on their places of worship." We asked respondents three questions:

1. How interested are you in learning more about the Faith and Solar initiative in Wisconsin?
2. Do you support or oppose increasing the amount of electricity Wisconsin generates from solar power?
3. To what extent do you agree Faith and Solar is an organization that shares your values?

The survey results showed that there were no statistically significant differences for the second (i.e., solar support) and third (i.e., sharing of values) dependent variables, regardless of the Muslim or Christian frame. This may indicate that community efforts to move to solar power can heal interfaith relationships as well as build a sustainable energy future.

Building on this ray of hope and light, our Wisconsin Faith Communities for Equitable Solar is gaining momentum. Wisconsin's Just Solar guiding principles are rooted in our collective values of justice, equity, and inclusion. We are generating energy from the people, by the people, for the people. It is time to light the way. The intensity of light is stronger in darkness. Let's continue to work together countering darkness and spreading light. Shine on!

Chapter Three

Building the Eco-Ethical Ark in the Age of Climate Disruption

Rev. Dr. Leah D. Schade

Science fiction writer Neal Stephenson wrote a book published in 2015 called *Seveneves.*[1] The premise of the book is that something explodes the moon into seven chunks that eventually begin colliding with each other, sending pieces crashing down onto Earth's surface. Scientists study the phenomenon and realize that eventually all the pieces will break into smaller and smaller bits, forming a white sky over the Earth. At that point, the pieces will begin falling in a cataclysmic event called "the hard rain" that will burn up Earth's atmosphere, boil its seas, and destroy all life on the planet. The scientists predict that humanity will have two years to put as many people and provisions into space as possible to preserve the human race and find a way for *homo sapiens* to survive for several thousand years until Earth becomes habitable again. This means they must put aside all of their differences of race, culture, religion, and socioeconomics in order to work together in building the "cloud ark" around the International Space Station. The first half of the book tells the story of this monumental effort through the eyes of several key characters charged with the task of overseeing this endeavor.

As I read this doomsday fantasy, I could not help but make comparisons to the *actual* apocalyptic scenario our planet is facing right now. Climate disruption, the sixth great extinction, the growing garbage patch in our oceans, the massive die-off of coral reefs, the loss of Arctic ice and the corresponding rise of sea levels, along with the increasing frequency of catastrophic weather events—all of this is a result of human activity. Our timeline may not be as short as twenty-four months, as it was in *Seveneves*, but scientists *are* debating how long the planet is likely to remain habitable for human beings—and it could be decades instead of centuries.

It is as if we are living in the midst of a dystopian science fiction novel of our own making. *We* are the hard rain. And we are bringing the planet to ruin.

17

I didn't used to be so blunt. For many years, I and others used the term "Creation Care" to instill a sense of moral and ethical responsibility into our discourse. It's as if we tried diligently not to offend or get too political with our rhetoric about issues that had become divisive and poisoned by partisanship. "Creation Care" seemed a viable term, for how can anyone take offence at *caring* about and for Creation? Plus, it has that nice alliterative ring: *C*aring for *C*reation.

But I've come to the conclusion that we need to expand and deepen our understanding of the phrase "Creation Care" so that it conveys the urgency needed to *act* on what is happening. I propose adding three other alliterative phrases: Creation Clarity, Creation Compliance, and Creation Compassion.

CREATION CLARITY

In July 2017, *New York* magazine published an article by David Wallace-Wells called "The Uninhabitable Earth." Wallace-Wells noted that the thawing of the Arctic permafrost is creating a feedback loop of global warming. He warned that the Intergovernmental Panel on Climate Change (IPCC) has overlooked key factors in its evaluations of the present and future of global warming. In frightening terms, he laid out the worst-case scenarios we will face from climate change. These include crop failures, increases in heat deaths, wars over resources, a surge of climate refugees, exotic diseases, unbreathable air, oceans unable to sustain life, and economic collapse.[2]

As a Christian homiletician, I have argued that preachers have a key role to play in helping congregations understand that attending to environmental and humanitarian issues is a matter of faith and moral/ethical obligation. Creation Clarity is needed to convey the necessity of addressing the climate crisis. Because of the sheer onslaught of raging fires, floods, droughts, and storms across this planet in the past decade, this is an urgent, all-hands-on-deck moment. Faith leaders need to step into the crisis to help elicit a depth of wisdom, insight, and motivation that can guide us, as individuals and as a society, toward a more peaceful, just, and Earth-honoring future. Preachers are uniquely positioned to present a vision of what is possible when the faith community addresses these issues and to clearly communicate what it means to live in right relationship with Earth, community, and God. This was one of the main tenets of my book, *Creation-Crisis Preaching: Ecology, Theology, and the Pulpit.*[3] Homilies and sermons are vital for the Creation Clarity we need right now, for they can raise awareness and help mobilize people for action.

But I must admit that most of the time, before I can begin describing the climate crisis, I find myself having to make the more basic case that Creation

Care is, indeed, part of our responsibility as Christians. Christian preachers often have to spend a frustrating amount of time playing catch-up, just helping people understand that the Bible authorizes Christians to address contemporary ecological threats. Meanwhile, the climate crisis is already well beyond our baby steps. So in addition to Creation Clarity, I believe we are at the point where we need to convey the message of Creation Compliance.

CREATION COMPLIANCE

Creation Compliance means accepting the urgency of learning to live in harmony with the rest of the created world. As a Christian, the words of Jesus keep echoing in my mind: "For those who want to save their life will lose it, and those who lose their life for my sake will save it. What does it profit them if they gain the whole world, but lose or forfeit themselves?" (Luke 9:24–25).

In other words, we must surrender to the calling of humility, obedience to the dictates of God's Creation, and a radical focus on building a just and equitable society and economic infrastructure that address the needs of "the least of these"—those who have particularly suffered under our oppressive reign. We need to stand with the people and animals being harmed on the front lines and advocate for and with them in the ethical dialogue and the halls of power. We also need to be imaginative about creating new forms of economic exchange.

From an ecofeminist perspective, all of this means attending to Earth as if it were our own body. Because, in fact, it is. This means attending to those most vulnerable as if they were our own selves. Because, in fact, they are.

I, for one, am willing to surrender to reality. I want our leaders and members of my species to accept Nature's terms. I want there to be Creation Compliance. I want us to survive. I want peace with this planet.

To aid in this Creation Compliance, scientists have developed a "roadmap" for meeting the Paris climate goals, which includes halving global emissions of carbon dioxide each decade, radically altering our planetary diet away from meat and fish and toward plant-based foods, and developing technologies and techniques such as carbon farming for drawing carbon from the atmosphere on a massive scale.[4] But all of this would have to happen within the next ten years in order for us to avoid the worst effects of climate change. Even knowing what we need to do, and the timeframe in which it needs to happen, something is keeping us from voting and acting in our own best interest.

There is a point in the *Seveneves* where some people cast doubt on the scientists predicting the hard rain. They think it's a conspiracy to undermine their country's sovereignty. They think it's all "fake news," and they ridicule the people who are preparing for what lies ahead. They try to continue with business as usual and scoff at the evidence that is right in front of them. Sounds familiar, doesn't it?

People's resistance to responding to the climate crisis is partly a result of the concerted efforts of the fossil fuel industry—and the politicians they fund—to confuse and mislead the public. But there is a psychological aspect to this resistance, as well. Unfortunately, human beings are not predisposed to think in global terms, or to conceive of time beyond a few years. Indian novelist Amitav Ghosh says it this way: "The dilemmas and dramas of climate change are simply incompatible with the kinds of stories we tell ourselves about ourselves, especially in novels, which tend to emphasize the journey of an individual conscience rather than the poisonous miasma of social fate."[5] In short, we need new stories: stories that activate our collective conscience and rally our global society to the task of salvaging what is left of our beautiful, precious, fragile Earth.

This leads to my third alliterative phrase: Creation Compassion. I think there may be another way for us to break through people's resistance to accepting the reality of our planet's condition and moving hearts and minds to take action.

CREATION COMPASSION—
BUILDING THE ECO-ETHICAL ARK

Neal Stephenson's characters in *Seveneves* called their interstellar refuge "the cloud ark." They drew on the archetypal story of Noah in the book of Genesis who heeded the warning about the impending flood and built a huge vessel to carry the remnant of animals and humans until the waters subsided. In our own time, I believe the ark to be the most plausible metaphor for the kind of project humanity must undertake in the decade ahead. We might imagine an "eco-ethical ark" as the metaphorical process that begins when people of differing faiths meet and connect philosophically, prayerfully, ethically, and with shared stories of compassion. This, in turn, can prompt us to work together to preserve the remains of precious life on this planet.

Our eco-ethical ark must be built with planks of the strongest ethical teachings of each religion, faith, and spiritual group. It must be supported with joists of justice and beams of righteousness. And the ark must be sealed by compassion that fills in the cracks and binds us together. The first ones on this ark must be the people and species who are most affected by climate change, especially indigenous peoples, people of color, islanders, fisherfolk hut dwellers, climate refugees, those living in poverty, and the plants and animals that are on the brink of extinction. As we build this eco-ethical ark, we must learn from those who have lived through and are currently suffering from the realities of the system's collapse. The colonialist traditions, the media executives, the advertisers, the rulers who have no heart for justice—all of them have had their time, and now their time is up. We in the wealthy West ignored the rest of the world as we created the problem; the time has come to repair what we have damaged and to cede our privilege and power to those with greater wisdom as we salvage what is left.

There is evidence that the frameworks for this eco-ethical ark are emerging. Organizations such as GreenFaith, Interfaith Power & Light, ecoAmerica's Blessed Tomorrow, and the Poor People's Campaign are doing important work to help build interfaith connections and organizational energy for what Thomas Berry has called the Great Work of our time. As I write this in early 2019, a group of bold legislators in Congress is proposing a Green New Deal that aims to address both economic inequality and climate change. My own interfaith work to fight fracking and a tire incinerator in Pennsylvania, and continuing now with Kentucky Interfaith Power & Light, has shown me that I have much in common with many Muslims, Jews, Buddhists, Sikhs, and those of other faiths—including those with no faith tradition, but who share the value of compassion. I relentlessly trust that in the midst of this work, we will discover that which will enable us to face the impending crisis. And I believe that thing to be the deep and abiding gift of *friendship*.

In the book *Seveneves,* only seven members of the human race survive the hard rain. The second half of the book imagines the world 5,000 years later. All religions have vanished, but a group of people emerges who believe in what they call The Purpose. While it is never defined in the book, I came to understand The Purpose as something mysterious that connects people with each other and with a fierce love of life that transcends horror and tragedy. The relationships and friendships among the characters join them to each other and to something bigger than themselves, enabling them to survive.

What I have learned through my own experiences with interfaith community organizing is that the precious bonds of friendship forged through struggling and suffering together for the causes of peace and justice are what empower me to move through the stages of grief and into acceptance of the human predicament. My friends in this work enable me to gain perspective and Creation Clarity. They give me the courage to prophetically proclaim the need for Creation Compliance. And these friendships are what ground me in Creation Compassion.

Jesus had special words about friendship. In John 15:12–14, he declared, "This is my commandment, that you love one another as I have loved you. There is no greater love than this, than one lays down one's life for one's friends. You are my friends if you do what I command you."

I think of those women who went to the tomb of Jesus to anoint his body after his crucifixion. Their friendship with him and with each other compelled them to show up because it was the right thing to do, the compassionate thing, the most loving thing they could do in the face of death and despair. We do the same. We do it not to be successful, but to be faithful, as Saint Mother Teresa of Calcutta once said. We pick up the hammer and nails to stand beside Noah and begin building that ark. We pick up the anointing oil and walk to the tomb to attend to the crucified places and people of this Earth. Who knows—perhaps in what began as a journey of despair, we will be surprised by whom we encounter there: the Divine One who meets us in our pain and transforms our personal and planetary wounds into eco-resurrection—places of healing and new life.

NOTES

1. Neal Stephenson, *Seveneves* (New York: HarperCollins, 2015).

2. David Wallace-Wells, "When Will the Planet Be Too Hot for Humans? Much, Much Sooner Than You Imagine," *New York* (July 10, 2017), http://nymag.com/daily/intelligencer/2017/07/climate-change-earth-too-hot-for-humans.html. Wallace-Wells later published *The Uninhabitable Earth: Life After Warming* (New York: Tim Duggan Books, 2019).

3. Leah D. Schade, *Creation-Crisis Preaching: Ecology, Theology, and the Pulpit* (St. Louis: Chalice Press, 2015).

4. Brad Plumer, "Scientists Made a Detailed 'Roadmap' for Meeting the Paris Climate Goals. It's Eye-Opening," Vox, March 23, 2017, https://www.vox.com/energy-and-environment/2017/3/23/15028480/roadmap-paris-climate-goals.

5. Quoted by Wallace-Wells, "When Will the Planet Be Too Hot for Humans?"

Chapter Four

Questions to Ponder
and a Spiritual Practice

QUESTIONS TO PONDER

1. All three authors—Mordechai Liebling, Huda Alkaff, and Leah D. Schade—have worked with interfaith partners in order to raise awareness about climate disruption and take steps to address it in their local contexts. Have you worked with interfaith partners in your own sphere of influence? Who are they, and what have you learned from them? If you have not yet had the opportunity to make these connections, consider reaching out to organizations such as GreenFaith, Blessed Tomorrow, and Interfaith Power & Light to join your efforts with a wider coalition of religious climate activists.

2. Each of the authors in this section points to scripture passages and holy teachings that ground their climate activism. If you are rooted in a particular religious or spiritual grounding, what are the sacred texts or teachings that provide the foundation for your work? Even if you are not affiliated with a specific religion, who are the teachers and religious leaders that have inspired you to put your values into action? What makes these individuals inspiring for you?

3. Frustration, burnout, and despair are challenges that each of these authors addresses in some way. Who are the people and what are the spiritual practices that have sustained you when the truth about the climate crisis threatens to overwhelm you?

A SPIRITUAL PRACTICE

Praying for Others

Praying for others gives voice to our interconnectedness with each other and with God. It allows the suffering of the world to enter our prayers. It expands our capacity both for compassionate connection and for letting go, as we entrust the ones for whom we pray to the mercy of God. Sometimes intercessory prayer can feel like reading a laundry list: we move so quickly or mindlessly through a list of names or concerns that we do not feel the divine Presence. This exercise invites us to stay in conscious contact with God as we uphold others in prayer.

Note: When practicing this exercise in a group setting, you will need a basket and slips of blank paper. The instructions can be read aloud.

- Pass around the basket that contains slips of paper. The leader invites each person to do the following: Take a slip of paper. Write your name on it. Fold the paper in half and hold it in your lap. . . . Place the empty basket in the center of the circle.
- Find a position on your chair or cushion in which you feel comfortable, relaxed, and alert. Close your eyes.
- Take a few deep breaths and allow your body to relax. . . . As you let the slip of paper rest in your open hands, spend some time becoming aware of the presence of God. . . . You might wish to imagine God flooding you with light . . . with vital energy . . . with compassion. . . . You might wish to repeat in silence, "Loving God, behold me."
- Give yourself to this prayer for a while. There is no need to rush. Notice whatever arises. Are you aware of any resistance to allowing God's love and light to flow into you? If so, gently acknowledge that, and, if you are willing, return your awareness to the divine Presence. . . . Allow it to fill you. . . . Invite God to behold you. . . . Take your time . . .
- The leader says Amen (or otherwise concludes this part of the meditation). Now pass the basket around and return the slips of paper to the basket. Mix up the slips of paper and pass the basket around once more, so that everyone picks someone else's name. (If you pick your own name, return it to the basket and pull out another slip.)
- If members of the group do not know each other by name, ask each person to say his or her name aloud.
- Hold in your open hands the slip of paper on which someone else's name is written. Close your eyes. Take a few deep breaths. Become aware of the presence of God. . . . You might wish to imagine God flooding the person

with light . . . with vital energy . . . with compassion. . . . You might wish to repeat in silence, "Loving God, behold this person . . ."

- Give yourself to this prayer for awhile. There is no need to rush. Notice whatever arises and return your awareness to the divine Presence. . . . Invite God to behold this person. . . . Take your time.
- Pause for a moment to notice that at the same time that you are upholding someone in prayer, someone else is praying for you. . . . How does it feel to know that someone is praying for you right now?
- Now let your breath bring to your awareness someone who is easy for you to love. . . . Pray for that person in the same way as you prayed before. . . . Rest in the divine Light.
- Now bring into your prayer someone who is neutral to you (for example, a neighbor, postal worker, or clerk at a store) and pray as before. . . . Rest in the divine Light.
- Bring into your prayer someone you consider an enemy, and pray as before. . . . Rest in the divine Light.
- Without planning in advance, let the breath bring to mind someone for whom you will pray. Pray as before. . . . Rest in the divine Light.

At the end of the meditation, people may wish to pair up to discuss what they noticed as they prayed for themselves and others, and what it was like to be prayed for.

Section II

RISING IN LOCAL ACTIVISM

Section II Introduction

This section features the voices of climate activists, with "boots on the ground," reflecting on their experiences from a faith perspective. While many of the other authors in this volume also have experience with direct action, we're bringing these three voices together with a specific focus. You'll notice that two of the authors—Fred Small and Shoshana Meira Friedman—write from different religious orientations about two protests against the same pipeline. Friedman's Jewish background and Small's Unitarian Universalist background offer contrasting perspectives, yet also demonstrate what it looks like to join across religious divides to protect a community. Jay O'Hara's chapter reflects on climate activism from the Quaker tradition. His chapter describes his experience blocking coal ships and walking a pilgrimage along a fracked-gas pipeline. All three authors reflect deeply on why they follow their chosen courses of action. As you read their chapters, notice the values that drive their activism and how their faith traditions hold them accountable to their neighbors and to future generations.

Chapter Five

Praised Be the Flood

Rev. Fred Small

I saw a sign recently. Well, I didn't exactly see it; I "saw" it on Facebook, which is as close to seeing as many of us get these days. It was the kind of sign you might see outside a general store or a muffler shop with hand-placed, all-capital letters, which in this case spelled: "HUMANS ARE 90 PERCENT WATER—BASICALLY CUCUMBERS WITH ANXIETY."

I thought that was pretty funny, so I posted it on my timeline, and immediately another Facebook friend whom I probably wouldn't recognize if they showed up at my front door posted a comment pointing out that actually, the human body is only 60 percent water. So of course, I had to Google "human body percent water" and found out they were right. But since we're in the realm of metaphor here, the exact percentage of water in our bodies isn't as important as the metaphor, which rings true to me.

Speaking for myself, I aspire to the serenity of a cucumber—with awareness.[1] But awareness carries terrible burdens. To be aware means to know that climate change is upon us, and that its first victims are mostly poor and of color—the most vulnerable people on the planet.

In the Turkana region of Kenya, for example, rising temperatures have ravaged livestock, fishing, and drinking water. "I don't know what climate change is," says one elder, "but I know from all the changes—the constant droughts, the seasons are gone—these are changes happening in our land. Our life is becoming hard, and we can't do anything. . . . I'll die anytime, but what of my grandchildren? I want them to have a future, but what are their lives going to be?"

His wife adds, "Maybe God knows how we'll survive."[2]

The years 2015 through 2018 were, until that time, the hottest in recorded history. In Antarctica, 2018 was *the* warmest year ever recorded, with alarming implications for sea level rise. Twenty-nine countries—among them

France, Germany, Italy, Greece, and the United Arab Emirates, where the thermometer hit 123 degrees Fahrenheit in June 2018[3]—experienced their warmest year ever in that year.[4]

That fall, the Intergovernmental Panel on Climate Change (IPCC) warned that we have only a dozen years to keep global warming to a maximum rise of 1.5°C, beyond which even half a degree would significantly worsen drought, flooding, extreme heat, and poverty for hundreds of millions of people.[5] To avoid this calamity, the IPCC said, "rapid and far-reaching" energy changes are needed.[6] Meanwhile, carbon dioxide keeps pouring into the atmosphere at unprecedented rates.[7]

Bill McKibben explains that to avoid catastrophic climate change, we have to stop all new digging and drilling for fossil fuels and stop building pipelines to move them, because the mines and oil and gas fields currently in operation worldwide already contain enough carbon to cook the planet. "From now on," declares McKibben, "anyone proposing a new pipeline, coal mine, [or] oil well is effectively a climate denier."[8]

While we're trying to put out the fire, President Trump is throwing gasoline on it, fast-tracking the Keystone XL and Dakota Access pipelines and appointing a fossil fuel zealot like Scott Pruitt to weaken and obstruct his own agency, the EPA. After Administrator Pruitt was forced to resign because he never saw an ethical violation he didn't like, his successor, former coal lobbyist Andrew Wheeler, has pursued the same pro-polluter agenda even more effectively.

Despite all of this, I still believe our fellow citizens are by and large basically good and decent people. We want to do the right thing. We want to help. There are entire professions and institutions whose mission is to help. The Coast Guard, firefighters, and first responders risk their lives—many would give their lives—to save mine or yours. And all of us—if we saw a child whose life was in danger—would help, wouldn't we? Wouldn't we do *something*? At least call 911 or maybe even do something heroic?

Yet how many children will die from climate change and the droughts, flooding, storms, famine, displacement, and disease that climate disruption will cause? And these same good, decent, sometimes heroic Americans don't do anything about it.

There are a lot of reasons. Ignorance. Ideology. Disinformation. Helplessness. Feeling overwhelmed. Despair. Economic insecurity. Addiction to the conveniences and distractions of hypercapitalism.

In the throes of addiction, no one can think clearly. No matter how loud the cries for help, addicted people who hear them are intoxicated; they can't think straight, let alone act. Twelve-Step programs tell us that few people will begin the hard work of confronting their addiction until they've hit bottom, their lowest point. Unfortunately, when it comes to climate disruption, if we wait until we hit bottom, that bottom will be a mass grave. Somehow, we have to break the trance and call our neighbors and ourselves into consciousness.

It won't be easy—far from it—but we can stop climate change. The tools are at hand: wind, solar, conservation, efficiency, smart growth, smart infrastructure, bio-agriculture, eco-restoration.

It is no longer enough to shrink our personal carbon footprint or to green our congregations. These are good things to do, but many of us have been doing them for decades, and the Earth has only grown hotter. We must take our prayers for Creation into the streets, into the voting booth, into the corridors of power. Personal transformation, community transformation, institutional transformation, and political transformation go hand in hand. None can succeed without the rest.

In the fall of 2016, I was arrested in an act of civil disobedience protesting the fracked-gas pipeline then under construction in West Roxbury, a neighborhood of Boston, where residents are worried about potential leaks and explosions, as well as about the pipeline's contribution to global warming. In solidarity with the Standing Rock Sioux in their struggle against the Dakota Access Pipeline, ten of us blocked construction in West Roxbury by either sitting on the edge of the trench or climbing down into it.

As the police arrested us, one of them whispered, "Thank you for your service."

They live there, too. They don't want the pipeline either.

Before the action, seventy of us gathered for interfaith worship at Theodore Parker Church in West Roxbury. We shared our grief for the Earth and all those suffering upon it. We prayed. We sang. Singer-songwriter Bryan Cahall performed his song, "Praised Be the Ragtime Band."

> Praised be the ragtime band
> Praised be the rambler's thumb
> Praised be the mislaid plans
> Praised be the flood if it comes
> Praised be the ragtime band
> Praised be our mislaid plans
> My eyes are dry and they are open
> I keep my grief in my hands[9]

"Praised be the flood if it comes." How do we praise the flood? How do we praise the flood that wreaks destruction, drowns our neighbors, and sweeps away everything in its path?

What if the flood is the breaking of the waters in the birth of a new world?

What if the cries of Creation are the labor pains of the birth of a new creation, a new society, a new way of being with each other and with ourselves—a way of compassion, a way of kindness, a way of justice, a way of healing?

What if the election of Donald Trump is an organ failure in the necessary death of systems, assumptions, norms, beliefs, traditions, aversions, addictions that no longer serve us—if they ever did—and do not serve life on this planet?

Valarie Kaur is an Indian American, a Sikh, a civil rights lawyer, and a mother. "What if," she asks, "what if this darkness is not the darkness of the tomb, but the darkness of the womb? What if our America is not dead but a country still waiting to be born? . . . What if this is our Great Contraction before we birth a new future? . . . Remember," Kaur tells us. "Remember the wisdom of the midwife: 'Breathe,' she says. Then: 'Push.'"[10]

Climate champion Tim DeChristopher reminds us, "Our old model of trying to meet all of our emotional needs with consumer goods hasn't worked. It hasn't made us happy anyway. Maybe greed and competition weren't the best values to be basing our society [upon]."[11]

Activist filmmaker Josh Fox adds, "The values that we will need to survive are deep inside of us, waiting to come out: courage, resilience, innovation, art, creativity, culture, generosity, community, human rights, democracy, the love of [our] fellow [human beings]. Those are the things climate can't change, and those are the things . . . we do [together]."[12]

The morning after Donald Trump was elected, Methodist pastor Steve Garnaas-Holmes wrote,

> When the temple falls we are awakened from the illusion that the world is just fine. . . . We finally know what others have known all along: we are vulnerable. We are exposed to the cynicism, violence, greed and hatred of the world. From the Roman Empire to the Holocaust to today's unarmed young black men, or the people of Aleppo, or refugees or the trafficked and exploited—they know: there is no guarantee of justice, no illusion that everything will be all right. The whole world is at risk. There is no refuge. There never has been.
>
> When the temple falls what do we do? When we can't look to our power structures, what do we do? We become the temple ourselves. . . . When the temple falls we become the resurrection. We let ourselves be raised, let ourselves be changed.[13]

So I invite you to imagine in your mind's eye a four-year-old child. It doesn't matter who it is. Maybe it's a girl in the Marshall Islands in the Pacific. Maybe it's a boy in an urban neighborhood in Sudan. Maybe the child lives here in the United States on the Gulf Coast or Long Island. Maybe she looks a little like your granddaughter. Maybe he reminds you of your best friend when you were a child. Imagine the shy smile on this child's face.

Imagine this child playing with friends. Imagine this child in the tender embrace of parents.

Now imagine that it's up to you whether this child suffers, whether this child is in pain, whether this child dies—from famine or drought or storm. From a flood that sweeps away her house. From water poisoned by contamination. From starvation in a refugee camp.

And now imagine this same child in a different future—growing up happy and well nourished. Sustained by family and community. Her world powered by renewable energy. Her path laid out with equal opportunity. Her voice being heard in a truly democratic government. These are the two futures before this child, before us all. Which future becomes real is up to us.

Is it too late to prevent climate change?

Of course it is. The damage has already begun. Some of it may be irreversible. Many will die. Many have died already.

But it is never too late to save the next life or the next species. It is never too late to offer love to our neighbor or even our enemy—never too late to feed the hungry, to welcome the stranger, to heal the sick, to visit the prisoner. It is never too late to repair the world. It is never too late to change.

There is no birth without death. In the Christian tradition, there is no resurrection without crucifixion. Everything is interconnected. All beings are our relations.

We are not victims of the flood. We are the flood.

"We are running waters," says Lakota activist Chase Iron Eyes. "Seeking a way, cutting fresh courses when spring swells us with power. We move mountains and break banks, creating."[14]

May we cut fresh courses. May we swell with power. May we move mountains and break banks until justice rolls down like waters, and righteousness like an ever-flowing stream.

NOTES

1. Serenity and awareness that are never fully attained in this life are desirable destinations of the spiritual journey. For us humans, it's hard to be both aware and serene. As a student of Thich Nhat Hanh, who advocated engaged Buddhism, I believe that awareness of suffering calls us to alleviate it. As a Unitarian Universalist, I believe that salvation and social justice are inseverable.

2. Abigail Higgins, "Climate Change Could Hurt Everyone. It's Already Devastating This Kenyan Town," *Washington Post*, January 30, 2016, https://www.washingtonpost.com/world/africa/climate-change-could-devastate-africa-its-already-hurting-this-kenyan-town/2016/01/29/f77c8e5a-9f58-11e5-9ad2-568d814bbf3b_story.html?utm_term=.dbd4a22b8b18.

3. "Weather: Maximum Temperature Touches 50°C in UAE," *Khaleej Times*, June 3, 2018, https://www.khaleejtimes.com/news/weather/weather-maximum-tem perature-touches-50c-in-uae.

4. Robinson Meyer, "The World Just Experienced the Four Hottest Years on Record," *Atlantic*, January 25, 2019, https://www.theatlantic.com/science/ archive/2019/01/nasa-noaa-shutdown-2018-warmest-climate-record/581221/.

5. Jonathan Watts, "We Have 12 Years to Limit Climate Change Catastrophe, Warns UN," *Guardian*, October 8, 2018, https://www.theguardian.com/environ ment/2018/oct/08/global-warming-must-not-exceed-15c-warns-landmark-un-report.

6. Daniel Aldana Cohen, "Apocalyptic Climate Reporting Completely Misses the Point," *Nation*, November 2, 2018, https://www.thenation.com/article/mainstream -media-un-climate-report-analysis/.

7. Meyer, "The World."

8. Bill McKibben, Twitter, September 23, 2016, https://twitter.com/billmckib ben/status/779342580479778816.

9. Used with permission. © 2010. Bryan Cahall. All Rights Reserved.

10. Valarie Kaur, "A Sikh Prayer for America on September 9th, 2016," valarie kaur.com, November 11, 2016, http://valariekaur.com/2016/11/a-sikh-prayer-for -america-on-november-9th-2016/.

11. Josh Fox, *How to Let Go of the World and Love All the Things Climate Can't Change* (2016), http://www.howtoletgomovie.com/.

12. Fox, *How to Let Go.*

13. Steve Garnaas-Holmes, "When the Temple Falls," *Unfolding Light* (blog), November 9, 2016, https://www.unfoldinglight.net/reflections/3839?rq=When%20 the%20temple%20falls%20we%20are%20awakened.

14. Connie GreyBull, Twitter, March 26, 2017, retweet of Chase Iron Eyes, Twit ter, March 25, 2017, https://twitter.com/search?f=tweets&q=%40chaseironeyes%20 we%20are%20running%20waters&src=typd.

Chapter Six

The Ground Beneath Our Feet

Rabbi Shoshana Meira Friedman

As the May sun bounces off the hard hats of the workers at the construction site, I ignore the approaching policeman, duck under the barrier with fifteen other faith leaders, and sit with my legs dangling in the pipeline trench. For the first time in weeks, my body relaxes. I smile, pick up my ukulele, and begin to sing.

The road to that act of civil disobedience began years earlier, back when climate change was still called global warming and I dreamed, quite literally, of saving the world. It was the mid-1990s, and the culture around me was full of the big environmental campaigns of the time—save the whales, save the rain forests, and that old favorite, "reduce, reuse, recycle." My elementary school's three central values were "Respect Yourself, Respect Others, and Respect the Environment," and that last one meant more than just cleaning up after snack time. It meant understanding and being attuned to the needs of the natural world around us. When my third-grade class took turns sharing what we wanted to be when we grew up, I said "environmental activist," and in those words made a sacred promise. In the way that only a small child can believe in her own power, I planned that by the time I died, all the world's ecological crises would have been solved by my future self's superhuman combination of scientific knowledge, charismatic leadership, and faithful activism.

Judaism also played a role in my early environmental consciousness. I was raised in a Jewish Renewal community that melded the heart-centered devotional practices of European Hasidism with the mid-twentieth century's values of egalitarianism, universalism, and environmentalism. I heard Judaism's central liturgy of the *Shema*—"Hear, O Israel, *Adonai* is your God and *Adonai* is One"—as Jewish language not only for the oneness of divinity, but also for the interconnection of life.

Throughout my teenage years, the goal to save the world from ecological collapse began to define my sense of purpose in life. But as my personal vision grew clearer, so did the enormity of the problem. News about the crisis only got worse. Overwhelmed by despair on a regular basis, I started to tune out news about environmental issues, debates, and disasters, and even success stories about smart policies and effective conservation. It all hurt too much to think about. And when I tried to take some kind of public action, I got stuck in self-doubt. What if it wasn't the right action to take? What if it wasn't effective? What if I failed? What if I inadvertently made things worse?

Still, that call wouldn't go away, so in 2001 I enrolled at Oberlin College as a Henry David Thoreau Scholar and declared an interdisciplinary major in Environmental Studies. I found a vibrant community of young idealists, revived my hope, and gained some skills. I worked with children over the summer at a nature camp, started a classroom garden at an elementary school, learned about the connections between agriculture and ecology, and steeped myself in the writings of transcendentalists for a college honors project.

After a few years of post-college jobs, I applied to graduate schools in natural resource management and policy. But something was missing. I hadn't reckoned with the well of pain inside me. My pull to environmental work came from a strong sense of empathy with the world around me—with people, animals, plants, and the land itself—and from an intense guilt over the toll it took on the Earth for me to eat, use electricity, drink and bathe, get around, and buy clothes. If I heard a news story about, say, mountaintop removal, I felt a punch to my solar plexus. I could feel the fear in the wildlife as the explosions rang out, the awesome grief of the mountain rent apart. And I knew I was complicit, part of the destruction. That knowledge caused more pain. I needed to pay attention to that hurt, to work in spaces and with people who could make room for it, and who would support me in living in alignment with my values.

One night, after helping to lead music at a Rosh Hashanah service, I acknowledged that policy work was not the right career path for me. I loved teaching, writing, speaking, singing, praying, and working in teams. I loved being present for people in important moments. I loved Judaism. I don't think I could have articulated it then, but I couldn't do social change work from a secular stance. The suffering and despair were too big. I needed religious community, my own Jewish tradition, and an inner orientation of service and faith. So I went to rabbinical school with the fervent hope that it would get me unstuck and started in earnest on my life's purpose.

Though I knew that environmental work needed to be a central piece of my rabbinic calling, I still got hung up on doubts, and none of my projects gathered momentum or felt joyful. During my time of study at Hebrew College, I had a spiritual direction session in which I shared the old pain with my spiritual director. She suggested I assemble a *beit din*, a rabbinic court of three of my most trusted teachers, and ask them to perform *hatarat nedarim* for me—a Jewish ritual for the nullification of a vow. In that sacred promise in third grade, I had committed myself to saving the world, which was something I could not possibly accomplish. So here I was, trapped, flailing inside the bonds of an impossible vow. During the ritual I told my story and cried. My teachers listened and recited back the liturgy in unison, "*Mutarim lach, mutarim lach, mutarim lach.* You are released. You are released. You are released." I felt a sudden release of energy from that place of pain in my solar plexus. None of us knew what would come of the ritual, but something had shifted.

A year later, Harvard Divinity School (HDS) invited me to speak on a panel about faith and climate change. I couldn't figure out how they had found me, but one of the coordinators of the event had heard me introduce a panel at Hebrew College on spirituality and the ecological crisis. It took a lot of *chutzpah* for me to accept that invitation from HDS. As far as I could tell, I hadn't done anything to earn being on a panel with religious leaders active in the climate movement. All I knew was that I cared about it. I took a breath, and accepted.

On that panel, clergy from other religious traditions—several of whom have articles in this book—explained that they do climate work not because they know they will succeed, but because working for a livable climate is how they witness to God's love for the world. It's how they show up with love for God and the world at this time in history. They do it because they are part of the first generation to feel the effects of climate change—and the last to be able to do anything about it. This was a revelation to me. It was all about *love*.

All these years I had felt blocked and overwhelmed, wanting to take action but getting stuck in fear of failure. And here were people—wise people, elders, and rising leaders in the movement—all explaining passionately that it wasn't about success. It wasn't about tactics. Of course, those were important, but they were not the actual ground beneath our feet. The only ground beneath us was the love we feel for the world and our desire to be in service to God, or Love, or Life itself.

This opened my heart and radically changed my life. Climate activism became a devotional practice for me, a form of prayer instead of a series of failed attempts at saving the world. The hours I have spent in relational meetings and in marches, on e-mail and on conference calls, crafting campaigns and speaking and singing at events—these have been hours of sacred service. They are my response to the suffering and to the crisis, and my response to being alive and grateful for my life. They are a way for me to serve God.

On the one hand, because there is no way to fail at prayer (as long as I have an intention of doing activism as a form of prayer), I don't need to worry about failure on a spiritual level. On the other hand, we are failing on the level of physics. The poor and marginalized suffer first, but we are all affected, so we are all called to awaken to our love and our strength. My activism lives in the paradox that in order to have the courage to effect any kind of change, I have to come from a stance of letting go of the outcome. I want us to be successful with all my heart, soul, and might, but if I waited for assurance of success before getting involved, I would never do a thing.

For many in the climate movement, myself included, this fight has become about defining our humanity. What does it look like to live up to my own ideals at this hinge-point in history? How can I help to grow a movement of people, committed to compassion and justice, who will take care of each other and of their neighbors as living conditions get harsher over the course of our lifetimes? How can we win on the front of the human spirit even as we are losing on the front of atmospheric physics? These are the questions that animate my activism.

In 2015 I joined a grassroots fight in West Roxbury, a neighborhood of Boston a few miles from my home. Despite a legal challenge from the City of Boston, Spectra Energy had received permission from the Federal Energy Regulatory Commission to build a high-pressure pipeline for fracked gas next to an active quarry and through a residential neighborhood. People got involved both because new fracked-gas infrastructure is bad for the global climate and because this pipeline posed a serious safety risk to the neighborhood. After exhausting all legal recourse, residents mounted a sustained campaign of nonviolent civil disobedience.

I decided to join the fight and to risk arrest. Wanting to leverage my position as a faith leader to have as much impact as possible, I spoke with close clergy friends and mentors in the interfaith community and organized a day specifically for clergy action. After many conversations, a lot of research, and coordination with community groups on the ground, we were ready. On the morning of May 25, 2015, sixteen clergy and religious leaders of eight different traditions gathered in front of the entrance to the metering and regulating station with about forty supporters. Before we marched to the construction site, I chanted the second paragraph of the *Shema* from a Torah scroll:

> If you listen, yes listen, to my commandments, there will be rain in its proper time. . . . [T]he land will give her produce. But if you turn aside from me and worship other gods, the sky will be blocked and there will be no rain. (Deuteronomy 11:13–17)

It was powerful to read these ancient words, so terribly relevant today, straight from a sacred scroll outside the gate. With Scripture in our ears, we marched, still singing, to the open trench where the pipeline was being built. The clergy ducked under the barricade and we sat in our vestments with our feet dangling in the trench. We prayed, sang, and testified until, one by one, we were hand-cuffed and led to the police transport vehicle. Inside the darkened vehicle and in the cell at the police station, we kept on singing. I felt a great peace. For at least one hour of my life, my whole body was engaged in this fight.

Unfortunately, we lost the fight to stop construction of the West Roxbury Lateral. But there is success in each act of human resistance to the disease of climate change. I remember the image from Paul Hawken's book *Blessed Unrest*—that we are part of an immune system rising up organically from the Earth itself. The response in West Roxbury was like the community mobiliz-ing to remove a parasite. From the standpoint of physics it's a failure that the pipeline went in at all, but it would have been an even greater moral failure if the pipeline had gone in without a fight. Our act of civil disobedience said that, even if the world is falling apart, we will not sit quietly on the sidelines and watch.

When my son was born at the end of 2017, I entered a new reality and a new universe of questions. Maybe one day I'll write an essay about decid-ing to have a child in a time of climate crisis. But for now, I can say that the energy and focus I had for activism and public life shifted dramatically with pregnancy and giving birth. I wonder: How do I work for a livable world for all when so much of my time and energy are devoted to sustaining life for one person, my child? Judaism teaches that to save one life is to save the world, and that each human being is a microcosm of the universe. Certainly, I have found that my love for my child has radically deepened my empathy with children everywhere—and with their parents. Yet it is still difficult to discern a good balance between serving my particular family and being involved in larger scale social action.

Being an activist awake to the pain of the world and a parent sensitized to the needs of my child are both daily practices in heartbreak and in giving and receiving love. Integrating the two is new and hard, and I am doing my best to face the challenge with curiosity. Recalling the image of the body's immune system, I'm reminded that no single cell can fight alone. These days, my deepest solace and strength come from connecting with other parents and activists, sharing our heartbreak, and walking together on the road of love—the surest ground beneath our feet.

Chapter Seven

The End of Hope and the
Beginning of Miracle

Jay O'Hara

The time for hope is over. Gone are the days of Al Gore urging us, from the glamor of the big screen, to change our lightbulbs. Gone are Nancy Pelosi and Newt Gingrich sitting on a couch, pledging that climate will be a bipartisan issue for action. Gone is the hope that a Democratic Congress and a Democratic president will propose—let alone pass—legislation that decarbonizes the U.S. economy.

Gone is the hope that a huge and powerful grassroots movement will spontaneously sprout and grow strong after a few catalyzing actions marked by effective organizing and persuasive messaging. Also gone is the idea that *I know* what will solve this crisis.

Gone is the hope that we have ten . . . or five . . . . or three years to avert the ultimate catastrophe. Gone.

As this fleeting and elusive hope disappears into the mist-filled gloom, grief looms in its place, and I admit that I am broken with despair. At the same time, I find that something else is arising: *faith.*

Of course, each moment of losing hope certainly didn't feel as poetic as that. I felt the loss of each hope intimately and painfully, as the external things in which I had placed my hope were smashed like waves of rising seas breaking against the rock of reality. Yet this experience is what opened me to a new understanding of faith. I have come to understand faith as relinquishing both the illusion of control and the expectation of success. Faith means to stare directly into the abyss and to walk into whatever it may hold. Walking forward in faith opens the door to a new possibility: the unexpected possibility that God may still have for us—the possibility of miracle.

And right now, when, according to the preponderance of scientific analysis, averting climate cataclysm is impossible, we need a miracle.

But what creates the condition for miracles? I can only describe it in the language of my Quaker tradition. We create an opening for miracles when we put away our own striving, our plans, designs, and strategies—in short, our ego—and decide firmly to worship only one God and to put nothing else above her.[1] It means to seek first the kin(g)dom[2] of God and know that all the other necessary things will be given unto you (Matthew 6:33).

This fundamental reorientation calls forth an authenticity and vulnerability that can bring powerful new things into being. This reorientation enables the risk-taking that is necessary in order to create significant change in the world. When divine power breaks into the life of an ordinary person, a new light breaks into the world. When that light comes to radiate through many thousands of us, there is no telling where it may go.

For this to happen, however, we have to make ourselves *available* to the Spirit. Right now, most of us are trapped in a domination system, an empire that wants to control us and is very good at doing so. I hear my parents' generation complain about how bad things are, yet they continue with their normal lives as if everything were fine. As for my own generation, I see my peers taking on things they can become mentally hostage to: debt, careers, mortgages, and children. How many times have we heard someone say, or heard ourselves say, "I wish I could make things better, but I can't—I'm too busy; I don't have time; I have too many responsibilities; I need to make more money"?

But the example of the path of Jesus leads us to move in a different direction. He invites us to reduce our burdens and trust that what is needed will be provided, just as it is provided for the lilies of the field and the birds of the air. He constantly reminds us not to store up our treasures, but rather to be alert and ready, for the call may come at any time. Twentieth-century Quaker Thomas Kelly put it this way:

> There is nothing more important now than to have the human race endowed with just such committed lives. . . . To this extraordinary life I call you—or He calls you through me—not as a lovely ideal, a charming pattern to aim at hopefully, but as a serious, concrete program of life, to be lived here and now, in industrial America, by you and by me.[3]

Even if we choose a path that seems likely to create positive change in the world, we still need to listen closely to where the Spirit is calling us, stay light on our feet, and be ready to change course. When I moved back to my hometown on Cape Cod in 2007 specifically to dig into grassroots climate organizing, I found myself not only caught up in the student climate movement in Massachusetts, but also launching a new program for college students. The "Climate Summer" program brought together small groups of students to learn and practice organizing for climate action across the state, all the while traveling only by bike, sleeping in church basements, and living on five dollars a day. The work was challenging and powerful. I had opened my life to be able to do this work because I had simplified my needs and could live on an annual income of about $16,000. I was working three days a week as a sailmaker in the local sail loft and was devoting the rest of my time to climate work.

The first year of the program, while not perfect, was productive, and the second year was shaping up well with a great new cohort of students prepared to arrive for training in June. But I felt unsettled. Just a month before the next training was to begin, I heard clearly within myself that this was not my work to do. I felt an inward stop that would not let me go. I realized that after months of feeling anguish and stress and of casting harsh judgments on those who didn't "get" the urgency of climate change, bad fruits were growing from a sickly tree. I realized that I was being called to a different path.

So I quit. I called a meeting of the three other people with whom I had been working most closely and confessed to them that I could not go on. In fact, the work was suffering because it was no longer my work to do. Thanks to this honest conversation, not only was an enormous weight lifted from my heart, but Climate Summer also continued successfully for five more summers, under the able leadership of my friend Marla Marcum, and accomplished more than I could have imagined.

Of course, at the time I had no idea what I was called to do next. But it seems to me now, looking back, that my inner spaciousness allowed me to experiment, to be flexible, and to make a transition from legislative advocacy and student organizing to the work that now feels authentically my own: direct action and climate disobedience. Clearing away those things that I "should" do and opening my life to the guidance of Spirit were the prerequisites for the civil disobedience to which I was eventually called.

A year and a half later, I was deep into discerning how to blockade coal shipments coming into Massachusetts. On May 15, 2013, my friend Ken Ward and I piloted our little white lobster boat named the *Henry David T.* into the ship channel at the Brayton Point coal-fired power plant, the largest single source of climate-changing emissions in the Northeast. While we only blockaded that ship for a day (and by some miracle were not arrested), we helped kick off a movement that called for the immediate shutdown of the plant. Ken and I were eventually charged, but, to our surprise, when we arrived at the courthouse, prepared for trial and surrounded by friends and supporters, the prosecutor dropped the charges. He publicly announced that our act of civil disobedience should not be prosecuted, because climate change needed urgently to be addressed. Whether because of activist pressure, the economics of coal, or a combination of the two, the plant closed its doors in 2017. Unexpected waves of transformation followed in the wake of one faithful act.

Pruning my life by clarifying and simplifying my desires made it possible to take the leap into this new level of faithfulness. Making specific, concrete changes in how we live and to what we give our sacred time and attention are prerequisites to making ourselves available to the immediate work of the Holy Spirit. Now I have the freedom to follow where the whispers of God beckon. I am free to improvise, to learn, to grow, and to experiment—in short, to be faithful.

The second major opening for me was discovering and stepping into a new kind of power. It is a power that comes through paradox, which lies at the center of faith. Kierkegaard argued that Abraham's faith consisted of being able to hold and believe two mutually exclusive truths at the same time: that he would kill his son Isaac because he would do as God commanded, *and* that God would fulfill the divine promise that Abraham would be the father of nations. This paradox applies to the work of climate justice as well. Giving up our ideas of being strategic is, paradoxically, the way to be effective. Admitting that we have already failed, and that we cannot know what is still possible to save, opens the possibility for authenticity. This, in turn, transmits empathy, connection, and the commitment that we need in order to be successful. Recognizing what we have already lost may give us the strength to do what is necessary to save what is left.

In April 2016, during the week leading up to Easter, my partner Meg and I, as part of a young adult group of New England Quakers, led a ten-day pilgrimage along the route of a proposed Kinder Morgan fracked-gas pipeline through Massachusetts and southern New Hampshire. Every day, between a dozen and fifty people braved the wintry weather, endured sleeping on hard church floors, and suffered sore muscles and copious blisters from walking.

It was distinctly a pilgrimage, not a political march. During the week, we focused on our own faithfulness and stayed attentive to our own need for transformation and repentance. We centered on worship and connecting with the local communities through which we passed. We didn't try to make the pilgrimage a "big deal" or to glorify ourselves. Instead, we focused on living in the Kin(g)dom of God through the community we had built within the pilgrimage itself, and within ourselves. In the course of that pilgrimage, we experienced faithfulness, deep joy, love, openness, and power.

Then, all those other things were added unto us. We were on the front page of every newspaper in the towns through which we passed. Reporters from TV stations in Boston came to cover the story of what we were doing. Other walkers appeared. Strangers offered assistance and kindness in the towns we visited. Houses of worship opened their doors and provided meals. Interested folks joined us in conversation and drivers tooted their horns. Those working to stop the pipeline were energized and encouraged. And after years of work by hundreds of citizens across three states, Kinder Morgan eventually withdrew its permit application.

By relinquishing our desire to control the outcome or to control other people, we realized that we didn't have to force others into some big plan about how this pipeline was going to be stopped. Instead, we found new powers arising within and among us. This pilgrimage took place because we sought not to vent our rage but rather to honor the pain in our hearts. We shared that pain and truth authentically, and as a result, people opened themselves to listen, to resonate, to empathize, and to join us in action.

When actions arise from conviction rather than calculation, from humility rather than arrogance, we feel and experience a power that comes from beyond our selves. I believe that this is the same power that made Jesus more than just another anti-empire, first-century radical. He manifested the paradoxical power of vulnerability. The paradox is that vulnerability is our strength. As Jesus taught, in order to have our life, we must lose it. In order to be a leader, we must be a servant. When we turn the other cheek, we upend a power structure that is based on domination and fear. And we discover that death on the cross is not defeat.

This power flows not from following abstract values found in the dead letter, even those in Scripture, imploring us to be good stewards of Creation, but from a lived reality of the Living Christ, the Holy Spirit that we experience within and that moves through us into the world. This power isn't always "pretty" and it doesn't always make sense. But I'm convinced that this holy vulnerability—the willingness to be a "fool" and to follow God's paradox in faith—is what opens the possibility for miracles.

Once I turn myself over to God, I find that taking action, whether that's making a pilgrimage or blockading a coal ship, is relatively easy. Once I have surrendered to the divine voice, then taking a risky act becomes a simple motion of faithfulness. And when I do act faithfully, I find the fruits of the Spirit poured over me, and I experience grace. As Dietrich Bonhoeffer professed and then exemplified, grace isn't cheap. If we want the authentic life of faith—transformation of ourselves and of the world around us (dare I say salvation?)—it won't happen unless we give up and give over.

Retirement accounts can't save us, social status can't save us, and those who counsel people not be "alarmist" are actually advocating for planetary suicide. So, I am left only with faith. My faith is in a Spirit that I trust will help us find a way forward. All I have to do is listen, discern, and hear where God is asking me to place my feet. I can only make myself available—then create the conditions that allow me to take those steps, and pray that my faithfulness may someday co-create the miracles we so desperately need.

NOTES

1. I refer to God using feminine pronouns to get us out of the rut of privileging male experience of the Divine.

2. The spelling of this word is deliberate and has a double meaning. "Kingdom of God" denotes the transcendence and immanence of God's reign "on earth as it is in heaven." "Kindom of God" suggests the immediacy and fullness of God's presence when we love our neighbors as ourselves—when we recognize that we are all members of one family.

3. Thomas R. Kelly, "Holy Obedience" (William Penn Lecture 1939, Arch Street Meetinghouse, Philadelphia, PA), http://quaker.org/legacy/pamphlets/wpl1939a.html.

Chapter Eight

Questions to Ponder
and a Spiritual Practice

QUESTIONS TO PONDER

1. Each of the authors in this section shares a story about courageous actions they took to protest powerful forces in the fossil fuel industry. Recall a brave step that you took toward fullness of life or a time when you made a decision to do the right thing, even though it was personally difficult or costly. What led to your willingness to take that step? How did taking that step change you?

2. Fred Small notes in his chapter that in the age of climate disruption, transformation is needed on all levels: "Personal transformation, community transformation, institutional transformation, and political transformation go hand in hand." Which of these levels is drawing you most strongly right now, and why? If you could take one action step in each of these areas to address climate change over the next six months, what would you do?

3. Both Shoshana Meira Friedman and Jay O'Hara talk about the doubts that can plague us when we consider taking action, as well as the discernment that is needed when we consider which actions to take and when we assess the wisdom and effectiveness of what we decided to do. When was a time you had to change course and reconsider a direction you had taken? What did you learn from that course correction? Who helped to guide you in a new direction, and what did they say or do that was helpful to you?

A SPIRITUAL PRACTICE

God in My Breath

This meditation is based on three exercises—"Body Sensations," "Breathing Sensations," and "God in My Breath"—presented by Anthony de Mello.[1] Like many practices that encourage silence and working with the breath, this meditation offers a way to steady and quiet the mind and open oneself to a larger awareness. Here is a suggestion: Take your time. The meditation has several parts, each of which stands alone and could be practiced fruitfully for a long time. Don't hurry to get to the end, but savor each step. Perhaps you won't complete the whole meditation because the initial steps prove so rich. That's fine. In a group setting, this meditation can be read aloud.

- Go to your sacred place.
- Find a position on your chair or cushion in which you feel comfortable, relaxed, and alert.
- Close your eyes.
- Take some time to ground yourself in your physical sensations. Let your awareness move slowly through your body. Be aware of the sensations in your head . . . your face . . . your neck and shoulders . . . your arms and elbows . . . your wrists and the palms of your hands . . . your back . . . your chest and belly . . . your buttocks . . . your thighs and knees . . . your ankles and the soles of your feet. There is no rush. Take your time.
- Bring your attention to your breathing. Become aware of the air as it enters and leaves your nostrils. . . . Let each breath come and go as it pleases, without trying to control it. . . . Feel the touch of the air as it passes through your nostrils. Is it warm or cool? . . . In what part of the nostrils do you feel the touch of air as you exhale? . . . Let your awareness rest in each breath. . . . Every breath is different. . . . When your mind wanders, gently return to the breath. . . . Let the breath become the anchor of your awareness.
- Reflect on the fact that the air you are breathing is charged with the power and the presence of God. . . . Imagine the air as a vast ocean that surrounds you . . . an ocean filled with God's presence. . . . As you draw air into your lungs, you are drawing God in. . . . Be aware that every time you breathe in, you are drawing in the power and presence of God. . . . God is breathing God's breath—God's spirit—into you. . . . As you breathe out, you are releasing the breath back to God.
- As you breathe in, be aware of God's Spirit coming into you. . . . Fill your lungs with the divine energy and compassion of God.
- As you breathe out, imagine that you are breathing out all your fears . . . your negative feelings.

- You may wish to imagine your whole body slowly filling with a warm, golden light.
- Conclude the time of prayer by slowly praying a verbal prayer from your tradition or a spontaneous prayer of your own.

As a variant to deepen awareness of God's intimate presence, you might try saying silently on the in-breath, "I come from You" and on the out-breath, "I return to You."

NOTE

1. Anthony de Mello, *Sadhana: A Way to God* (New York: Image Books, Double-day, 1984), 15–16, 26–27, 36–37.

Section III

ROOTING SCIENCE AND POLICY IN FAITH AND SPIRITUALITY

Section III Introduction

Climate activism takes many forms. Some people choose to lift protest signs or chain themselves to fences to raise awareness about the dangers of pipelines or to put a halt to the fracking industry encroaching on a community. Others express their activism through educating in the classroom, writing books or blogs, or sending letters to the editor of the local newspaper. Still others invent new technologies, explore new kinds of economies, or find more efficient and Earth-honoring ways to grow food or make buildings. There are countless ways to make a meaningful contribution! In this section we bring together three climate activists working within the fields of science and policy. What makes these authors unique is the way their faith informs their vocation as scientists and/or public health officials. Katharine Hayhoe, Natasha DeJarnett, and Corina Newsome each share how their values, grounded in their Christian upbringing, lead them to care deeply for the communities—both human and Earth-kin—that suffer from the impacts of climate change.

Chapter Nine

The Imperative of Hope

Dr. Katharine Hayhoe

I'm a climate scientist. Every day, I look at what's happening to our planet; and what we see in the data is disturbing, concerning, and even frightening.

This fear is spreading throughout our professional community. At scientific conferences, we still present esoteric treatises on the analysis of foraminiferal records and internal variability in multi-model ensembles, but now, there are also presentations simply titled, "Is the Earth F*cked?" Satire hits close to home, like the *Onion* article describing "a weary group of top climatologists [who] suddenly halted their presentation . . . , let out a long sigh, and stated that the best thing anyone can do at this point is just try to enjoy the next couple decades as much as possible. . . . [So] they would be skipping the remainder of the conference to get completely shit-faced at the nearest bar."[1] When I shared this with a roomful of climatologists and asked, "Who's with me?" 40 percent said they were right behind me; 20 percent said they were already there; and the remainder said they just suppress their anxiety.

What we see in our scientific work is the very opposite of hopeful. So it's no surprise that "What gives you hope?" is one of the most frequent questions I'm asked.

For hundreds of years, we've been living as if there's no tomorrow. We're running through our resources to the point that today, we'd require five or six planets if everyone in the world were to enjoy the lifestyle of a middle-class North American: producing enormous amounts of waste that are polluting the Earth's air, water, and land that we all share and depend on, and disrupting the Earth's natural carbon balance to the point where, unchecked, the resulting climate change will put our entire civilization at risk. The poorest and most vulnerable among us already disproportionately suffer the consequences of these choices today and, all too soon, our choices will harm us all.

I study climate change because, at its core, it is a humanitarian issue. It exacerbates the problems we already face, from poverty to hunger—even political strife and refugee crises. As climate scientists, we're like physicians who have diagnosed a disease that affects the entire human race. The Earth is running a temperature. It's our lifestyle choices that are the cause. And we know that if we continue on that current pathway, the consequences will be severe and, ultimately, dangerous.

Like physicians of the planet, I believe we have a moral responsibility to tell people what we've discovered. This task alone is enough to bring one to despair. Often it seems as if every new study that comes out finds that climate change's impacts are happening faster or to a greater extent than we thought: sea level rise doubling, ocean heat uptake increasing, ice sheets shrinking, impacts multiplying.

Our communication challenge is exacerbated by the way the cautious, measured warnings of scientists have been disregarded and even dismissed over the last few decades. Those guilty of doing so include politicians, decision makers, and the public at large, most of whom may largely agree that the climate is changing and that humans are responsible but are convinced the risk is minimal. We see this around the world, where policies to preserve our common home play little to no role in elections other than as a backlash against what are perceived to be liberal or globalist tendencies.

Not only that, but when we speak up about what we're witnessing, we're often subjected to an avalanche of hate. For me, the majority of it doesn't come from people who are so antithetical to who I am that I can easily dismiss them. Rather, much of it comes from those who profess to share my values and my faith: the Lutheran pastor who told me I was just in it for the money; the Christian student who told me that "believing in anthropogenic global warming makes you a sinner," and advised me to "get familiar with Genesis"; the woman whose social media profile reads, "If the world hates you, know that it has hated me before it hated you," and then went out of her way to find me, express her hatred of me, and only block me after she was sure I'd seen what she had to say.

Today, climate change denial is part of a toxic package of identity issues. This mindset can manifest itself in many ways: a retreat into rigid and legalistic orthodoxy, whether religious or political; hostility toward or even dehumanization of those we feel are "different" than us in terms of gender, race, or culture; conspiratorial thinking that dismisses real issues in favor of imagined threats; and a raging anger against any and all who are perceived to stand in our way. But the roots of this toxic brew are all the same: *fear*. Fear of change, of loss, of me not having what I believe I deserve, of others getting what I think they don't deserve.

Those bearing the brunt of these attacks are also afraid: afraid of the results of this short-sighted mindset, of the harm it may do to us personally, and in the case of climate change, the fact that it puts the entire future of humans on this planet at risk. This can overwhelm us with anxiety and despair. One colleague shared with me that she can't mention the words "climate change" in class, because one of her students will have a panic attack. With other colleagues, I studied hundreds of undergraduate students and found that, after they read a book and attended a lecture about climate impacts and how much had to change in order to fix the problem, they became even *less* engaged and concerned than they were before.

As humans, our emotional bandwidth is limited. That's why, long term, we need hope, not fear, if we are to solve this problem. All too often, fear merely triggers rage, a desperate and ultimately futile attempt to hold back the tide. Or fear makes us feel anxious—as well as inadequate, that we cannot influence the problem ourselves—and eventually detached, if we feel we can't do anything to fix it.

"We do not accept climate change because we wish to avoid the anxiety it generates," George Marshall writes in his book *Don't Even Think About It: Why Our Brains Are Wired to Ignore Climate Change*.[2] And psychologist Renee Lertzman goes even further, pointing out that talking about climate can challenge some of our most deeply held beliefs and fears—which we typically deal with by avoiding.

Without hope, there is no reason to continue. So where do I look for this hope? Not to my science, but to my faith.

"For God has not given us a spirit of fear," the apostle Paul tells Timothy, "but of power," to act; "of love," to have compassion—for those who are different from us, those whom we perceive as standing in our way, and most of all, those who are already suffering today; and "of a sound mind," which enables us to make decisions informed by the reality of what is happening in the world around us (2 Tim. 1:7).

Over the last few decades, climate change has become one of the most polarized issues in the world. Today, our political identity is the best predictor of whether we believe what thermometers say. Yet our opinions do not alter reality, and it's our own future that's at risk if we convince ourselves they do. As Leonardo da Vinci said, "The greatest deception men suffer is their own opinions."

The reality is that we've known for more than 150 years that burning coal, gas, and oil produces heat-trapping gases that are building up in the atmosphere, warming the world. We are conducting an unprecedented experiment with our planet, and our civilization is completely unprepared for its impacts: on our food, our water, and the places where we live. Since the

1980s, we've already averaged five billion dollars per year in crop losses due to climate change, much of that occurring in the poorest countries in the world. Many of our freshwater resources are already overallocated, and warmer temperatures only increase demand. The coastal zone is home to trillions of dollars of infrastructure and hundreds of millions of people, including two-thirds of the world's largest cities. How can we prepare ourselves for what the future holds?

Without hope, scientific projections will become a self-fulfilling prophecy. But what that verse in 2 Timothy tells me is this: If my response to the science I study is fear, then that is not of God. And that's why, in my personal search for hope, I begin with my faith.

What is the purpose of our faith? It isn't a vague abstraction, a belief that somehow everything will work itself out. The Christian faith is solidly aimed at a target: God, and what He has done for us. In Romans 5:1, Paul makes it clear: By faith, he says, we have been justified or made right. We have peace with God and, even more, we have access to the grace or undeserved merit with which we stand before God (Romans 5:2). Through this faith, we "glory in tribulations, knowing that tribulation produces perseverance; and perseverance, character; and character, *hope*"; and this hope "does not disappoint." Why? Not because of any action of our own, but rather "because the love of God has been poured out in our hearts" (Romans 5:3–5). The source of my hope is my faith, and this hope will never be disappointed because it is based on the foundation of the one who will never leave us or forsake us (Hebrews 13:5).

The apostle Paul was specific in the nature of his hope and its purpose. In today's world, we, too, need specific hope. We want to know—What I can I do? Is anyone else doing it? Is it possible to fix this thing? The answers to these questions are what will spur us—and others—to act.

When we actively seek out, aggressively pursue, and seize this hope with both hands, we can find it: whether it's record-breaking low prices for solar energy, cool new technology, or inspirational stories of people doing unexpected things where we live or on the other side of the world. There are companies like Swiss Climeworks or North Carolina's Net Power that are building carbon-neutral power plants; army bases like Fort Hood in Texas switching to solar and wind energy to save money and cut carbon emissions; faith-based leaders from Interfaith Power & Light's Sally Bingham to the World Evangelical Alliance's Bishop Tendero advocating for and modeling change; and students like Greta Thunberg from Sweden or Tina Oh from Canada pushing for fossil fuel divestment. I'm encouraged by each of these stories and look for more like them every day.

As a Christian, I believe I am called to love others with the love that God has given me; and through persevering through tribulation, we arrive at hope: a hope that we can hand the planet to our children and grandchildren in better shape than we found it. By working together, we can find hope, not fear—the power to act and not despair. Together, rooted and grounded in the love that powers our hope, we can transform the very fabric of our society and tackle this enormous global problem that is climate change.

NOTES

1. "Sighing, Resigned Climate Scientists Say to Just Enjoy Next 20 Years As Much As You Can," *Onion*, February 23, 2018, https://www.theonion.com/sighing-resigned-climate-scientists-say-to-just-enjoy-1823265249.

2. George Marshall, *Don't Even Think About It: Why Our Brains Are Wired to Ignore Climate Change* (New York: Bloomsbury, 2014), 229.

Chapter Ten

The View from My Window

Natasha DeJarnett, PhD, MPH

I remember gazing out my childhood window in Georgetown, Kentucky, one spring afternoon in 2007 just as I was ready to move away to graduate school. Trees filled the landscape—maple, ash, redbud, and oak reaching for the endless blue sky, towering over neighbors who walked their dogs and chatted with each other as they strolled the streets that framed the lake. Flowerbeds adorned the hillside—tulips, day lilies, and daffodils. On my desk were pictures I had taken of these flowers—the details of their petals and leaves showing the generosity of God. The idea that God puts that amount of attention into one single flower and gives us millions of them amazed me. As I stood by the open window, I felt the breeze on my face and heard the sound of children laughing outside. I imagined they were chasing each other across the yards as I did with my friends when we were kids. From my window, I could see hope and a future.

A decade later when I visit my childhood home, the landscape through that window has changed remarkably. The lake is shrinking. A quarter of the trees are gone, killed off by extreme weather events and a devastating ash borer infestation. Many of the beautiful flowers have disappeared because they no longer have shade.

I have changed in these ten years as well. My knowledge and understanding have expanded now that I have completed my master's and PhD in public health, studying environmental health. My postdoctoral fellowship concentrated on air pollution and heart disease, which led me to explore the intersection of climate change and public health. Gazing out the window today, armed (and sometimes burdened) with additional insight, I wonder what my future children will see from this window. Will they see the beauty I experienced in my childhood, or will climate change continue to alter the landscape? Beyond that, I wonder how it will affect their health. Will I hear them outside laughing, chasing each other up and down the hills? Or will climate-related health threats prevent them from sharing the experiences that I enjoyed?

My role in addressing climate change and health has largely been to inform policy. This means that I educate. To leaders in public and environmental health and policy, I provide educational tools that equip them to make informed decisions on policies to protect health as the climate changes. In addition, for the general public, I provide education that I hope will build a groundswell of advocates who will call on their policy-makers to act on climate change to safeguard health. These tools may consist of developing content for fact sheets or infographics, organizing a webinar, or writing papers. For me, it's exciting to take the latest scientific information and put it in terms that the general public can understand—to explain the problem of climate-harming pollution and what we can do to defend public health. I also apply a lens of equity to my climate-related work, examining how climate change worsens disparities for certain groups and assessing policies to ensure that they don't have unintended consequences on vulnerable populations.

I've often heard it said that we are the first generation to experience the impacts of climate change and the last that can do something about it. For my part, I'm seeing those impacts from climate change in the form of severe threats to public health that worsen preexisting health conditions and exacerbate health inequities. Extreme heat is increasing the incidents of asthma and heart diseases and raising the risk of heat-related illnesses such as heat exhaustion and deadly heat strokes. In fact, extreme heat is the top cause of weather-related deaths in the United States. Extreme heat is an occupational hazard, threatening the health of people in the construction and agriculture industries. And although extreme heat-related deaths are more preventable compared to other climate impacts, people without access to places where they can cool off on a hot day are the ones who particularly suffer. This is especially the case for people living in impoverished communities and communities of color, and those who are socially isolated, like the elderly or people with language barriers. Also at risk are vulnerable children playing outdoors or living in homes without air-conditioning.

Climate change decreases the quality of the air we breathe. Dirty air is deadly air. Poor air quality is linked with higher mortality, and higher levels of air pollution are associated with shorter life expectancy—meaning that people who live in more polluted areas have shorter lives. Each year, seven million people die worldwide because of air pollution. Poor air quality increases our risk of chronic conditions like respiratory and cardiovascular diseases. Air pollution is an added burden for communities of color and impoverished communities because they are more likely to live on the fence lines of industrial polluters or near highways with tailpipe emissions. These communities already experience a higher risk of heart disease, diabetes, and asthma, and exposure to air pollution worsens these conditions. Additionally, longer, hotter warm seasons cause longer and more intense pollen seasons, which is bad news for allergy sufferers. Allergies can result in missed school and work and can induce asthma complications.

Gazing out my window, I think of climate experiences that have shaped my life. One extremely hot summer afternoon stands out. My parents and I were gathering very large, heavy rocks to construct a stone walkway. We were in a largely unshaded area on a hill, right off the interstate. I remember Mom saying she needed to sit down. I recall noticing that she was sweating profusely, like nothing I had ever seen before. She was short of breath, although she was sitting. Dad decided that she needed shade and water. When I looked in her eyes, I saw something I'd never seen in her before: helplessness. My mother is the strongest and most determined woman I know, but the look in her eyes let me know that something was seriously wrong. Realizing that the shade wasn't immediately helping, I wondered if her life was slipping away. I couldn't shake the terrifying thought of life without my mom—the woman who gave me life, who held my hand and kissed me when I was sick, who hugged me and told me she loved me every single day, whose attention made me feel that I was the only person in her world, and the woman who taught me to pray.

Once Dad was able to get her some water, she started cooling off and feeling better. But she could have easily become another heat-related fatality statistic that day. The toxic combination of extreme heat, plus strenuous activity, along with the poor air quality induced by the traffic emissions from the adjacent highway created a perfect recipe for my mom's condition. This experience underscores my quest to halt global warming and prevent others from seeing their family members face climate-related health challenges.

In my work, I emphasize that communities must find ways to help citizens adapt to the changing climate in order to protect public health. That means we need accessible cooling stations for extreme heat days, poor air quality alerts, and evacuation plans that enable all vulnerable populations to be transported to safety during extreme weather events. In addition to taking action steps to adapt, we must also advocate for climate change mitigation strategies that will reduce the release of pollutants and safeguard our health from further climate harm.

What's most alarming to me about the threat of climate change is the imbalance in the burden borne by those who suffer. Threats to public health affect everyone; however, some groups are more vulnerable than others. Ironically, those who have contributed the least to creating the climate crisis are the ones most burdened by it—children and the impoverished. The World Health Organization reports that 88 percent of the burden of climate change falls on children under age five. That statistic is heart-wrenching because it lays bare our collective failure to provide a healthy planet for children and future generations.

As a person of color who suffered from asthma attacks as a child, this reality hits home for me. My summers visiting my grandparents down South in Alabama filled me with many great memories—playing tag in the backyard; really, *really* good food; and the warm hugs of grandparents. But there were challenges, too. I noticed that whenever I visited my grandparents, my otherwise well-controlled asthma would flare up. In graduate school, I had the opportunity to explore my hunch that my asthma attacks and the air quality in North Birmingham, Alabama, were related. I selected that community as the site of an environmental health assessment project for a class.

I learned that the community had been filled with air- and soil-polluting steel mills until the mid-1970s. Discriminatory housing practices meant that this was one of the few places in which African American families could reside. Therefore, my grandparents were subjected to both housing discrimination and environmental racism. My research revealed that their community had higher risks of asthma, heart disease, and low-birth-weight infants. While there are many complicating factors that intersect in these health problems, environmental factors play a significant role. I learned a little more about my purpose through my assessment of my grandparents' community. I discovered that my desire to improve the health of vulnerable populations is underscored by my quest for justice. I believe that no one should be burdened by an unhealthy environment. I want everyone to be able to look out of their window and see healthy environments and, most importantly, find reason to hope.

It was my dad who taught me the importance of putting hands and feet to that hope. I remember joining him for voter registration drives. We would walk door to door throughout the most oppressed neighborhoods in central Kentucky. Even on days where we added only two new voters to Kentucky's registry, Dad would be glowing with pride. He'd say, "That's two more people who are able to use their voice through their vote and make a difference." This experience inspired me to be the voice for the voiceless and disenfranchised. As I have grown in my profession, it has taught me to ensure that the oppressed find and exercise their own voice, that the underrepresented have a seat at the table. My calling to fight climate change to protect health means that I must uphold justice. Sometimes I find it overwhelming to consider how climate change inequitably threatens the health of communities suffering from environmental injustice, like that of my grandparents or the oppressed neighborhoods where we registered new voters. But I can't stay in the mindset of despair.

Instead, I must remember that the people in the communities where my grandparents lived need me to do my work and my research to help improve lives. They also taught me that people are resilient. Communities like that of my parents' birthplace have survived the Great Depression, racism, riots, and even violence. They have been making a way out of no way for generations. And they will overcome the challenges of climate change, too—through prayer, action, and lifting our voices together. Rev. Dr. Martin Luther King Jr. challenged us, asking, "What are you doing for others?"[1] I can proudly declare that I am raising the visibility of the voiceless in the climate change movement to improve their health and quality of life.

Looking through my childhood window, although the landscape has changed, my hope has not. Nor has my responsibility. We are called to be good stewards of this Earth, this beautiful gift. Just imagine the amount of time God puts into the exquisite beauty of a small flower. I recall one childhood Christmas where we spent the morning opening gifts. I had received so many beautiful clothes and delightful toys, all that I could have hoped for and more! But after the gift exchange was complete, I took my new treasures to my room and tossed them on the floor. My mom passed by my room and said, "That's not how you treat a gift—you don't just throw it on the floor." I hadn't intended to show ungratefulness toward my gifts. Similarly, many of us don't intend to destroy this beautiful gift that God has given us, but that is what we're doing. Undoing God's great work runs counter to the will of God. The undoing is also a deep disservice to future generations. I feel a keen responsibility to act on climate change because failure to take action is a form of neglect for the health and well-being of future generations. One verse has echoed throughout my life, "To whom much is given, much is required" (Luke 12:48).

The view from my window is a small indication of all that God has given to me and all of us. God has given us the minds and hearts to find the solutions to climate change. In doing this work, we must be grateful, mindful, prayerful, and dedicated to taking action—for faith without works is dead. We must tap into the resilience that our communities possess. It's the resilience to register voters and empower democracy to make positive change. It's the resilience to watch family members suffer and to use that suffering as an impetus to learn, study, and improve the health of others. It's the resilience to take a family member's ailment and see it as an opportunity to turn empathy into policy to protect today's children—and generations to come.

So when I look out that window, I don't just see what *is*. I also see what is *possible*.

NOTE

1. Martin Luther King Jr., quoted in Gabriela Landazuri Saltos, "MLK, Jr. Asked Us 'What Are You Doing For Others?' Here's How We Answered," *HuffPost*, January 19, 2015, updated December 6, 2017, https://www.huffpost.com/entry/mlk-day-serving-others_n_6489236.

Chapter Eleven

The Thing with Feathers

Corina Newsome

"Hope" is the thing with feathers—
That perches in the soul—

—Emily Dickinson[1]

My hometown of Germantown in Philadelphia, Pennsylvania, was, in many respects, bleak. There was minimal green space, and as a result, very little observable wildlife. Growing up in this poor, heavily urbanized area of Philadelphia, I didn't have many opportunities to look closely at the details of Creation. But I did have my grandma's *National Geographic* magazines. I always asked her to send them to me once she was finished reading them. With each new stack of magazines, I met new people from every corner of the Earth. I saw flowers and lemurs and dangerous jellyfish. The picture of the Masai Mara National Reserve in Kenya didn't exist only as a picture in the centerfold: I felt its heat and life. Looking at the pages of these places I hadn't been, and things and people I hadn't seen, didn't make me unhappy with my circumstances—but I knew I wanted to see the natural world for myself. So, when the time came, I decided that I would make a career out of my desire to look closely.

Before attending college at Malone University, an Evangelical Christian school, my academic study of natural science always existed separately from my faith; they were incompatible. Years of observing the reactions of other Christians to the natural sciences—namely, the exclusion of God from scientific explanations—molded my worldview in such a way that I believed that studying the physical was an active denial of the mysterious work of the Divine. Thankfully, during my college studies I encountered professors and mentors who provided a safe and healthy framework in which I could engage in thoughtful criticism of those worldviews. After deconstructing the barriers

69

that sequestered my faith from my studies, I was joyfully surprised to find the character and essence of God woven through every detail of the Creation that He spoke into existence.

In one of his addresses to Israel, the prophet Isaiah offers a wonderful image: "The mountains and hills will burst into song before you, and all the trees of the field will clap their hands" (Isaiah 55:12). This text is situated within a description of the redemption to be experienced by those who returned to the Lord, and it reminds me of the restoration I experience whenever I stand in God's sanctuary of the mountains, hills, and trees. When I am gripped by troubling thoughts and emotions, I thrust myself into the greenest space I can find, and I sit still. I know that, due to the precariousness of life, the survival of each living thing I encounter seems to hang almost constantly in the balance. Nevertheless, they burst with beauty, detail, and a very specific set of tools that allow them to persist for another moment. In surrounding myself with the richness of these truths, I find peace.

Toward the end of my undergraduate studies, I took a field course in ornithology, the study of birds. I never had any particular interest in birds, so I was not thrilled at the prospect of having to learn to identify more than 150 of them. On the first day of class, my professor, Dr. Jason Courter, began with an introduction to the ten most common bird species in our area of northeast Ohio. He started with a species well known to many: Blue Jays. When their picture was displayed on the board, I exclaimed, *"That species lives here?"* I had never seen one before. There were very few species of birds where I grew up in Philadelphia, and I barely noticed the ones we did have. But meeting the Blue Jay was all it took—I have been captivated by birds ever since.

In the sanctuary of the outdoors, I look for birds. They remind me of hope. In the most desolate landscapes, whether barren from human destruction or naturally harsh, you will find birds that have discovered a niche in which to survive. And if you travel to the most biologically diverse and thriving ecosystems, you will find birds varying in brilliant color, free to evolve the most captivating adornments and behaviors. They remind me of the presence of God: "If I ascend up into heaven, thou art there; if I make my bed in Sheol, behold, thou art there" (Psalm 139:8). In seeking out and studying birds within God's sanctuary of the natural world, I discovered a restful and restorative hope bursting with life that perched gently in my soul.

I am now continuing my studies in ornithology as a graduate student at Georgia Southern University, focusing my research specifically on the conservation of birds threatened most immediately by climate change. As a student of the natural world, this hope I speak of is mixed with a strong sense of urgency. I am acutely aware of the global crises resulting from human-caused global warming. This warming results in drastic environmental changes that are happening so quickly that many species are unable to adapt. Although this is a desperately sad and discouraging reality to accept, there is one bit of hope: the same humans whose activity caused this unprecedented damage to the Earth have the potential to stop this destruction from running its full course. Still, it's clear that taking the necessary collective steps to bring such a reality to fruition has proven to be a battle on many fronts.

One of those fronts is within the church itself. Historically, Christians have been a large, diverse group of change agents with a deep commitment to the Word of God and to living out the Gospel. I assumed, then, that I could count on my fellow believers to act on climate change. As the truth about the state of the natural world began to unfold for me during my studies, I was filled with a sense of purpose: I wanted to bring all that I had learned to the church. I thought to myself, "If they think they are amazed by God now, wait until they look closely at what He created!" This would necessarily lead to a desire to actively steward the Earth's resources as we were commanded in Scripture, right? Though I had never heard such a conversation take place within the walls of any church, I believed I was just the person to make it happen.

Disillusionment was waiting for me at the door. Back home, the churches in my neighborhood were surrounded by deep-seated issues stemming from generational poverty and racism. The effects were visible everywhere, whether on the streets or in the pews—problems like poor healthcare, broken families, drugs, homelessness, hunger, and weak educational systems. When I implored my church family to consider the natural world and God's call for us to steward our resources wisely and live more sustainably, I discovered that other problems took priority. If you don't know how you will feed your family tonight, reducing your use of single-use plastics is hardly a concern. If you can't be at home with your children because you have to work multiple jobs just to keep the electricity turned on, reducing your carbon footprint by carpooling to work is not on the to-do list. I was discouraged when my message was thwarted by these realities. But what could I say? Dealing with immediate challenges had to take precedence over other concerns.

By contrast, the churches in the neighborhood of my university were predominantly white and upper middle class, with a few poor college kids sprinkled in the mix. Surely these people would have no excuse to opt out of the mission for preserving God's Creation, I thought. But a new kind of discouragement awaited me there.

I felt this disillusionment most keenly during my senior year of college while attending my best friend's bridal shower. Attempting to get a rise out of me, someone laughingly shouted, "Hey, Corina! That guy threw all of those recyclables in the trash!" He stirred up a few chuckles. Then, a wealthy and highly regarded member of the local faith community asked me, "Corina, do you believe that God created the Earth?" Confused, I responded, "Yes." Condescendingly, she retorted, "Well, don't you think He can take care of it?"

This time, I wasn't just disappointed: I was hot with anger. The sad part is that I knew from experience that she wasn't the only person who thought like this. Are we, the keepers of the light, the shouters of truth, the proclaimers of hope, so misled as to believe that we have no responsibility to occupy this planet in a sustainable way? Are you, as privileged, white Americans so padded by your comforts that you clutch your pearls at the thought of living as God instructed us to? For the short remainder of my college career, my frustration existed as stagnant rage. I decided that the church was a lost cause and a waste of energy. I became intimately familiar with the truth that "hope deferred makes the heart sick" (Proverbs 13:12).

My heart was so sick, in fact, that I almost missed an important opportunity to connect my faith with my care for God's Creation. The same professor who introduced me to the Blue Jay invited me to attend a conference on our campus hosted by an organization called Young Evangelicals for Climate Action (YECA). At first, I had no interest because I assumed that because they were Evangelicals, they likely came from the same demographic that had so enraged me. But on the morning of the conference, I felt a sudden urge to attend. I vividly remember sitting in the conference, tearing up as I witnessed an impassioned group of people my own age encouraging us not to give up on the church. They urged us to encourage our faith communities to join this movement to address our collective impacts on the planet's warming climate.

As I listened, I realized they were bringing me a new perspective. Yes, God instructs us to steward the Earth. But the climate crisis forces us to have a multidimensional understanding of that ethical requirement. Acting on climate change and protecting the natural world is a necessary extension of God's command to *love our neighbors as we love ourselves*. When we recklessly consume and waste materials, casting them into landfills out of sight, that waste ends up polluting the living spaces of our sisters and brothers in poverty. When we continue to mindlessly produce greenhouse gases as we live and travel, the resulting changes in the climate exacerbate natural disasters, and the most vulnerable among us are the first to suffer from those impacts. While this information was not new to me, it wasn't until that moment that I realized how working to mitigate both climate change and the destruction of the natural world was deeply and necessarily integrated with my faith. It seemed that it was possible, after all, to return to the church with this call to action.

After pushing past the anger, hurt, and hopelessness that I felt regarding the lack of climate action in the church, I am now participating in that very mission more fully than I ever imagined was possible. Overcoming that hurdle was one of many situations in which I have experienced hope after moving beyond my comfort zone. Four years after my first encounter with the people of YECA, I now sit on their steering committee. I've come to firmly understand that acting on climate change is an issue of faith . . . and *justice*. Yes, climate change harms people, and is caused by people. But the hope for solutions to this problem lies within people.

I continue to find this hope as I discover individuals and groups working in the background and foreground of the climate justice movement. People are using their spheres of influence and privilege of access to hold church and political leaders accountable. People in frontline communities—those that are most immediately and intensely affected by the impacts of climate change and environmental degradation—are crafting solutions that meet immediate needs for survival while also improving quality of life. An example of these efforts that deeply resonated with me was the JUST Energy conference in Atlanta, Georgia, in 2018. Hundreds of African Americans and allies to our community gathered to boldly identify the ways in which the energy system has historically disenfranchised poor black and brown people—from the unjust, forced use of black bodies to power European exploits in North America, to building power plants in locations that contaminate our backyards. But we didn't stop there. Together, we brainstormed ways in which we can position our communities to be beneficiaries of the new clean energy movement, and break the cycle of toxic, unjust energy production.

I've come to learn that within the climate justice movement, both hopefulness and hopelessness are present in equal measure. This presents me with choices. I can choose hopelessness, knowing that certain humans are actively working against the ability of threatened communities and species to survive. Or, I can find hope in our collective commitment to climate justice and environmental restoration. When I walk through my neighborhoods back home, I can choose hopelessness when faced with the reality that every one of us has had to fight simply to meet our daily needs. Or, I can find hope in our resolve to fight for our communities in the face of dangerous environmental change. When I walk into the church, I can choose hopelessness when I recognize selfish theologies and misguided pursuits. Or, I can find hope in the Good News of redemption and in the knowledge that we are, in fact, not alone in our efforts to bring justice and restoration to fruition.

As I seek refuge in the forested hills and refreshing sanctuary that God's Creation provides, I take comfort in this: there is no place I've gone where hope has not found a way to survive and perch gently in my soul.

NOTE

1. Emily Dickinson, "'Hope' is the thing with feathers" (c. 1861), in *The Complete Poems of Emily Dickinson*, ed. Thomas H. Johnson (Boston: Little, Brown, 1960), #254, 116.

Chapter Twelve

Questions to Ponder and a Spiritual Practice

QUESTIONS TO PONDER

1. Hope is a strong theme among the writers in this section. Katharine Hayhoe, for example, observes that fear can lead to the extremes of hatred or despair, neither of which leads to the kind of actions needed to address climate change. She insists that hope born out of faith can counteract those negative extremes and allow us to develop fresh approaches to tackling the climate crisis. What are your sources of hope? If you are a person of faith, what teachings or Scripture passages convey this hope most strongly to you? If you do not practice a faith tradition, what cultivates hope within you? How do you convey hope to others?

2. Communities of color are especially hard hit by climate change issues. As the chapters in this section elucidate, air pollution, environmental toxins, and extreme weather events exact a heavy toll on neighborhoods already struggling with poverty, crumbling infrastructure, lack of access to good healthcare and nutrition, and neglected education systems. What is one policy change you can work for in your community that will address climate change as it intersects with the disenfranchised and those caught in cycles of economic struggle? Consider connecting with the Poor People's Campaign (https://poorpeoplescampaign.org) to learn more about how you can join with others to address the intersections of poverty and environmental issues.

3. Both Natasha DeJarnett and Corina Newsome list specific flowers, trees, and birds that they have come to love, but also mourn, because of accelerating habitat loss and species extinction. What is a species of plant or animal you have loved that is adversely affected by climate change or en-

vironmental harm? What steps can you take to advocate for these members of the Earth community who are among "the least of these"?

A SPIRITUAL PRACTICE

Kinship with Creation

Many of us experience Earth and other creatures as entities that are separate from us. Many of us—especially we who are city dwellers or who spend hours every day on a screen—feel no particular connection with the living world around us or with the other beings with whom we share this planet. Yet the insights of science accord with the wisdom of religion: human beings do not exist in isolation. We exist within an interconnected web of relationships. This meditation invites us to exercise our imagination and deepen our understanding of our place in the universe. How would our behavior change if we were more keenly aware that we are brother-sister beings with the rest of life and spring from the same divine Source? In a group setting, this meditation can be read aloud.

- Go to your sacred place.
- Find a position on your chair or cushion in which you feel comfortable, relaxed, and alert.
- Close your eyes.
- Notice that as you breathe in, you are taking in oxygen, which is released by trees and all green-growing things. As you breathe out, you exhale carbon dioxide, which in turn is being taken up by trees. Breath by breath, you are exchanging the elements of life with plants. . . . As you follow your breath, let yourself feel your connection to the air, and to trees, and grass, and everything green.
- Now let yourself feel the weight of your body in the chair. . . . Notice your connection to the earth. You are as solid as the earth, and made from the same atoms of carbon, oxygen, hydrogen, and nitrogen that make up the earth. To the earth, in the end, your body will return. . . . As you feel the weight of your body in the chair, feel your kinship with the earth.
- Now let yourself sense the inner motions within your body. . . . Maybe you are aware of gurgling in your belly or the throb of your beating heart. Maybe you sense the circulation of blood as it moves through your body. Most of the weight of your body comes from water, just as most of our planet's surface is made of water. Your blood is mostly water, and the saltwater content of your blood's plasma is the same as the saltwater content of the sea. It is as if within your body you are carrying rivers, lakes, and

the ocean. Let yourself savor your body's kinship with all fresh waters and with the sea.

- Now scan your body. Get a sense of your body as a whole. You have considered how your breathing connects you to the air, and to plants . . . how your body connects you to the earth . . . and how the waters inside your body connect you to the planet's waters and seas. . . . Now consider this: all the elements that make up your body came from stars that exploded millions of years ago. . . . Your body is made of the same elements—the carbon and nitrogen—that circulated through all the creatures that have ever lived, far into the distant past, and that will circulate through any beings that inhabit the world far into the distant future.
- Our bodies connect us to the air and to plants, to the earth, to waters and the sea, to the animals, and to the stars.
- Let yourself appreciate the goodness of the amazing body that God has given you and feel your kinship with the whole Creation.

Section IV

RISING FROM THE MARGINS

Section IV Introduction

The climate justice movement is a civil rights movement. Just as Rev. Dr. Martin Luther King Jr. once shared his dream for this nation about the end of racial inequality and injustice, so people of faith in the "green" rights movement also have a dream. We dream of clean air and land and water and of a world where humans live peacefully with each other and with the Earth upon which all life depends. Just as the Civil Rights Movement of fifty years ago was animated by the power of churches and synagogues, this "Green Civil Rights Movement" needs people of faith to provide moral and ethical authority, to frame caring for God's Creation as a matter of justice, and to rouse the incredible power within our worshiping communities to address the climate crisis. The three authors in this section—Peterson Toscano, Gerald L. Durley, and Lennox Yearwood Jr.—are noted civil rights activists who find points of intersection with the environmental rights movement and climate activism. Toscano draws lessons from the fight for LGBTQIA rights, while Durley and Yearwood connect the legacy of racial justice to the climate movement. Each of them—and their respective communities—brings unique gifts from historically underrepresented and oppressed communities that provide key insights and wisdom for engaging in climate activism today.

Chapter Thirteen

Not Our First Rodeo

Memory and Imagination Stir Up Hope

Peterson Toscano

"Put these on." Ron, my boss and the owner of the ambulance company that I worked for, handed me a mask, a pair of latex gloves, and a thin, cotton jumpsuit lined with a film of plastic. The elastic cuffs of the jumpsuit's sleeves and ankles clamped over the gloves and around my socks. With booties over my shoes and my eyes shielded by protective gear, I was completely covered. It was 1984, and I was transporting an HIV/AIDS patient to a hospital in New York City, one hundred miles away. I was nineteen years old.

The patient, thin, with deep, hollowed-out eyes, looked like a Jewish Holocaust survivor from a picture in a history book, except that he was black and this was not his liberation. He lay in silence, staring with those big eyes as the driver and I lifted the stretcher into the back of the ambulance. No one yet knew exactly how the sickness was transmitted, so patients like mine received the full hazmat treatment and were quarantined in hospitals, as caregivers shrouded in protective gear flitted in and out as quickly as possible. Many of the early HIV/AIDS patients spent the rest of their short lives with no one touching their skin again, as a lover would, or a mother, or a friend. Untouchables, they were the modern outcasts.

I closed the ambulance door behind me, shutting me in with my patient. I sat far from him, near the door. We never exchanged a word during the two-hour trip. We just made eye contact from time to time. What did I see in those eyes? Fear? Shame? Anger that he was being moved again and treated like a biohazard that no one dared to touch?

Two years earlier experts had called the disease GRID, the gay-related immune deficiency. In the media they called it "gay cancer." Some preachers proclaimed it was "God's punishment against homosexuals." I learned about it from newspapers and TV. All the first-reported cases involved young gay men in New York City and San Francisco. As a young Christian man, I was terrified by the gay desires I felt and was desperately trying to ignore. This strange new sickness multiplied my fears.

"There but for the grace of God, go I?" I wondered. If I embraced being gay, would I, too, end up like this man—despised, rejected, hidden away, and quickly fading? Still, I understood that even if I did contract HIV/AIDS, no matter how awful my last weeks on Earth would be, this black man had already suffered more than I ever could. We might be in the same boat to-gether—AIDS victims—but not on the same deck. Many hospitals turned patients away and funeral parlors routinely rejected victims' bodies, but even with the horrors of HIV/AIDS, some people suffered more than others depend-ing on their access to healthcare and on the discrimination they faced because of race, class, gender, sexual orientation, and other socioeconomic factors.

Months later I plunged into my studies at a small, Christian liberal arts college outside of New York City. By sticking my head in the Bible and focusing my daily prayers on begging God to keep me from falling into "the gay lifestyle," I kept myself aloof from the HIV/AIDS crisis. I spent the next fifteen years immersed in church, all the time asking God to open my eyes, while at the same time averting my gaze from the realities I did not want to see—my own sexuality and the struggle for survival and equality for which LGBTQ people were fighting so hard—people I actively rejected.

Finally, at age thirty-three, I came to my senses and came out as gay. I had to build a new life with a new identity. Emerging from denial and fear, I was propelled into public speaking, political theater, and other forms of LGBTQ activism. Ten years later, I met Glen Retief, a South African living in the United States who taught creative writing at a small liberal arts college in rural Pennsylvania. We found a kindred spirit in each other, fell in love, and became a family. With marriage equality finally becoming a reality and with the Obama administration making moves to pursue legal equality for trans-gender people, I felt confident in letting go some of my LGBTQ activism and queer Bible scholarship.

Then in 2012 the reality of climate disruption crashed into my life. It was Glen's fault. As a distraction from writing and grading papers, he strayed into reading about the science of climate change. Like a seed hidden under-ground, swelling, and rising to the surface, his concern grew about the rapid changes that were taking place because of global warming. I knew nothing of his growing despair until the day I found Glen weeping in the bedroom. "It's about climate change," he explained. "It's worse than they imagined. It's happening faster than they feared. We have to do something."

With his help, I began to see climate change as an issue that is bigger than South Africa's apartheid, the LGBTQ movement, and the American black Civil Rights Movement combined. I experienced apocalypse—a soul-jarring revelation. I saw that we are poised on the brink of a massive human rights struggle that will affect everyone on the planet. Glen helped me recognize that climate change is not just a scientific issue or an environmental concern, but something that affects people differently, depending on the discriminations and prejudices they already experience. As temperatures rise, storms, droughts, and heat waves multiply and magnify, and with them so does human suffering. Crop failures and destruction of property can affect all of us, but some of us have the social and financial means to find other sources of food and to rebuild or relocate, whereas others, whose options are already limited, find their troubles multiplied and their options running out. Climate disruption is like the AIDS crisis: we may all be in the same boat, but we are not all on the same deck. Class, race, geographic location, gender, sexual orientation, and socioeconomic factors will stratify the suffering among us.

The monstrous challenges presented by climate change remind me of what early HIV/AIDS activists faced. I began to study the history of our society's response to this epidemic and learned how the U.S. government initially refused to act. President Ronald Reagan, inaugurated in January 1981 just as the HIV/AIDS crisis emerged into view, did not speak publicly about HIV/AIDS until 1987. The public was frightened and growing increasingly hostile. Hate crimes against LGBTQ people rose dramatically. AIDS patients died in a matter of weeks, often in their homes after hospitals refused to admit them. People directly affected by the illness endured enormous suffering, while the general public knew hardly anything about it. The media mostly ignored the story or stoked fear and hatred, instead of raising awareness and engendering compassion. The situation seemed hopeless, and those who were suffering felt powerless.

Then the LGBTQ community did something extraordinary: they *acted up*! Activists—mostly people in their twenties who had never before participated in public protests—organized, educated themselves, documented the crisis, lobbied government officials and agencies, and stirred up support from medical professionals. They made noise. They shut down government buildings. They paraded their dead friends through the streets when funeral homes wouldn't bury the victims. They provided healthcare in each other's homes, they delivered meals, they washed clothes, and they cradled their friends and even strangers as they died. Perhaps most importantly, they broke the collective silence. No one was talking about AIDS, so in order to get the story out, they demonstrated, they wrote articles, they created plays, films, and art. They designed the AIDS ribbon, the very first ribbon fixed to a lapel to raise awareness about an issue. They constructed a giant quilt that covered the Washington Mall. They told themselves and the world, "Silence=Death." They persisted in getting the word out until the world took notice.

These activists not only humanized the people suffering with HIV/AIDS, they also changed systems. Patient-doctor relationships in the United States were forever transformed because of the patients' rights movement initiated by AIDS activists. What's more, their work led to the development of new drugs that are saving millions of lives today. Their art and activism serve as a model for us today in our struggle to awaken the world to the urgent need to address climate disruption.

When it comes to the climate crisis, I remind myself—*this is not our first rodeo*. AIDS activists are an example of how human beings can rise to an existential challenge and meet it with extraordinary compassion, organization, and commitment to justice. Earlier generations of activists show us that as a people and as individuals, we have faced and survived countless trials that seemed poised to defeat us. In many cases we did more than simply ride out the storm and survive: we emerged wiser, stronger, and kinder. Of course, there is no guarantee that hard times and suffering will bring out the best in us; they often reveal the worst in us, too. Still, when I look at history, I am amazed at the many times that human beings overcame our worst instincts and ended up doing something selfless and loving. In so doing, we also pursued ambitious solutions that saved lives. All of us, whatever our background, come from a people who have changed the way the world operates.

I think, too, about another time in history. In the early 1940s, the city of Leningrad was under siege by the Nazis for almost 900 days. Bombs fell from the sky four times a day. Women and children, along with the elderly, were cut off from electricity and gas lines. Fires erupted from the bombs and from the makeshift fires that citizens lit in their apartments in a desperate effort to stay warm. In a single month, January 1942, more than 100,000 people perished. By February, 20,000 people were dying every day. Miraculously, many survived that desperate first winter of the 900-Day Siege.

After the bombing of the food warehouse that held their precious rations, the citizens had to take matters into their own hands. They began planting gardens everywhere. They used overturned tables filled with dirt to plant lettuce and cabbage. In between bombings they dug up courtyards and planted rows of beets and potatoes. By November 1942, they had produced a four-month surplus of food.

But it's not just the past that gives me inspiration. I also use my imagination to envision a better future in order to catch a vision of hope. I perform a stage show called *Everything Is Connected—An Evening of Stories, Most Weird, Many True*. I share with the audience some of human beings' greatest accomplishments, and I also invite the audience to consider where our ancestors got it wrong. Can we learn from their mistakes as well as from their successes? And what can we learn from the future?

The show finishes with a character who is distraught, angry, and frightened about climate disruption. He is dismayed by society's inaction to address the crisis. He then reveals that he has received a comforting word from an unlikely source. "I've been hearing voices lately," he confesses. "Well, not voices, exactly. I guess I've been hearing messages from people in the future, like one hundred and two hundred years in the future. They are trying to tell us something." He looks out at an audience member: "I keep hearing them say, 'Thank you!'" He turns to someone else and says, "Thank you," and to someone else, "Thank you for everything you did for us!" He scrunches up his face, looking puzzled, and in a voice full of emotion concludes, "So I'm thinking, what the hell are we about to do that they are going to thank us for?"

As a person of faith, I need to imagine success. In fact, I actively engaged in considering our success as human beings when I wrote fifty monologues set in the year 2165, about 150 years in the future. I created the character of a climate historian whose job was to convey to the public the stunning achievements of a group of people known as "the climate generation." He recounts the stories from 2015 to 2035 of how *our generation* took on climate change, broke through society's collective silence, and changed systems. As I wrote these monologues, my vision expanded to consider how much is possible and how even the most unlikely people already have the values and experience to make unexpected, positive contributions.

People ask me, where do you see hope? What keeps you from giving up? I see within all of us the potential to love deeply and pursue solutions, regardless of party affiliation, class, or religious background. Time and time again we have risen to the occasion. Under pressure we have often surprised ourselves and discovered resources deep within ourselves that we had no idea we possessed.

Climate change is often called a threat multiplier, for it tends to exacerbate other threats, such as poverty, the violation of human rights, and war. Will climate change also magnify and multiply our human tendency to respond in fear, so that we ignore pleas for help, build walls, and selfishly bunker down and shut out the world? That may be, but we also carry within ourselves a capacity for compassion. In recent decades we have witnessed the extraordinary loving-kindness of neighbors and even strangers who bring comfort to those in need, be it in the aftermath of a terrorist attack in lower Manhattan, in an air raid shelter in a besieged Soviet city, or from a loving caregiver who wraps up an AIDS victim to keep him warm, hold him close, and love him to the end. No, this is not our first rodeo, and just like the other rodeos that came before, we need the same thing: love—fierce, fearless, selfless love. As threats multiply, so must our humanity, so must our love.

Chapter Fourteen

Confronting Climate Change

Wisdom from a Civil Rights Activist

Rev. Dr. Gerald L. Durley

When I was initially approached about contributing an essay on this timely topic of climate change, I hesitated as to whether I was ready to publicly share my long-standing personal feelings and struggles that have accompanied my lifelong struggles for justice. I questioned whether I could muster my internal voice to speak up and out about atrocities against people who are being denied their civil and human rights because of climate change. As I mulled over the theme "Voices of Courage in a Time of Climate Crisis," I realized that the civil rights challenges I have faced all my life—and that continue to be a menacing threat—are now compounded by the complexities of global warming. Yet it is facing challenges like these that has given my life meaning and purpose.

As a young African American growing up in the 1950s in a relatively poor neighborhood in Bakersfield, California, I learned to pick cotton, cut grapes, box tomatoes, sack potatoes, and pick peaches in the company of "undocumented human beings" from Mexico. That was a way of life. We boarded the labor transport bus at 5:30 a.m. and worked all day in the sweltering California heat. Seldom did I understand the spoken language of my co-workers. Yet, I felt a strong sense of human connectedness. We were merely attempting to earn money to improve our lives. It was not lost on me that I was a teenager who had a home to which to return every night, while many of my co-laborers slept in pickup trucks or in overcrowded motel rooms. This experience more than fifty years ago helped to lay the foundation of my becoming a lifelong civil and human rights advocate.

There are events, moments, and circumstances in all of our lives where, either knowingly or unknowingly, we reach a critical turning point—we begin to become conscious of our need to find a meaning for our lives. Working closely with people who endure and overcome seemingly insurmountable odds helped me build my character for the "play of life" in which we all play our role.

Looking back, I see that I actually experienced a minimal amount of overt racism in Denver, Colorado, where I completed high school. Classmates of Mexican and Asian heritage were an integral part of our diverse community. But that changed after graduation when I was recruited to play basketball in Nashville, Tennessee. The transition from the West to the very different culture of the South in 1960 brought me swiftly to my search for meaning. Until my sojourn to Nashville, my life was not complex. My *goals* were simple—get an education and play professional basketball. But my *purpose* in life was as yet undefined.

I soon learned that one's purpose is determined by influences that impose themselves on one's thoughts and shape one's behavior. Before Nashville, I was naively oblivious to how the stark, harsh realities of segregation and racism affected me personally. But in Nashville that changed, and my life's purpose was born as a result of experiencing blatant racist behavior. I became an active participant in the Civil Rights Movement. I embraced Dr. Martin Luther King Jr.'s clarion message: "Injustice anywhere is a threat to justice everywhere." I began to speak up and to speak out against inequitable conditions and treatment imposed on those considered to be the least, the left out, the left behind, the forgotten, the abused and harassed populations in America.

Witnessing acts of immoral discrimination against innocent human beings fostered in me a drive and courage that was fed by my need to initiate and sustain service to a cause greater than myself. Understandably, segregation triggered anger, fear, and loathing in me. I had to learn to sublimate these negative emotions so that I could express my purpose effectively—without assaulting others or taking actions that would have been counterproductive to my purpose. I channeled these negative feelings into positive efforts like picket lines, organized rallies, peaceful marches, and public speaking. Through them all I stayed true to my purpose of advocating for civil rights. I participated with devoted courage and commitment to a cause that affirmed my meaning.

I went on to live and work in Africa and Europe for a few years. I eventually returned to America to continue to promote the cause of those I was committed to serve. I became a dean at Clark Atlanta University, and the pastor of the historic Providence Missionary Baptist Church of Atlanta, Georgia. As a pastor, psychologist, and civil/human rights advocate, life was progressing well. I had reached a plateau, and it seemed that things were at peace. That was when God shook the core of my existence.

In 1996, God introduced me to a person who had committed herself to confronting the teenage pregnancy crisis in Georgia. Her name was Jane Fonda, and she, too, had found her purpose in life. She was an advocate who had exemplified courage throughout her adult life. We joined our commitments to pursue justice and to champion the cause to reduce the teenage pregnancy rate through the Georgia Campaign for Adolescent Power and Potential.

During our work together, she introduced me to members of her family who were passionate about keeping the environment clean for human, animal, and plant life. Her family was committed to putting an end to the causes of global warming and to decelerating climate change. Their goals were to propose and implement laws for environmental justice—a cause they encouraged me to become a part of. This chapter was not in my life's original plan. At first, I could not see a connection between civil rights and climate change. It took some time, but I began to understand how environmental issues were connected to the economic, educational, emotional, and spiritual needs of those I served.

Jane ignited my quest for amplified meaning, and introduced me to Laura Seydel, Ted Turner's daughter. Laura is an ardent activist for saving the environment. Through their tutelage, I was reenergized to adopt an expanded purpose for my life. Meaning will find you when it is ready. You do not have to search long—it will find you.

I began to learn from Laura about the causes and consequences of global warming. I started to read and understand how climate change was affecting the lives of those whom I was called to serve. I learned new terminology, such as *acidic oceans*, *fossil fuels*, *greenhouse gases*, *bleached coral reefs*, *food deserts*, and *fracking*. I was shocked to find out that the atmosphere on which we depend is being destroyed, and that I had been oblivious to it. I began to pay attention to extreme changes in weather patterns and to the devastation of hurricanes, tornadoes, floods, droughts, earthquakes, massive fires, severe cold, and excessive heat. All of this was being studied and debated among scientists, climatologists, business people, politicians, and environmentalists. But there was minimal discussion of these issues in my faith community.

Scientific surveys and published data reported that changing weather patterns were having a disproportionately negative impact on rural, low-income, and minority communities. It became clear to me that those who contributed the least to global warming suffered the most as a result of climate change. Loss of employment, limited healthcare, destruction of houses, long-term illnesses, and death were just a few of the problems I discovered that challenged members of these communities.

I then met Reverend Sally Bingham, the founder of Interfaith Power & Light. Reverend Bingham patiently connected the dots for me in terms of what God intended for us to do with this ecologically balanced world that was entrusted to humankind. I came to a new understanding of what was written in the book of Genesis 2:15, where God commanded that we be good stewards of the Earth. I recognized that the civil, human, and constitutional rights of the people most harmed by climate change were being denied because of the overt greed of fossil fuel companies and the policy-makers they fund.

I eventually grasped the importance of this movement. Through my commitment to placing global warming, climate change, and environmental justice at the center of my mission to serve, I found a renewed meaning for living. The consequences of not acting *now* create a sense of urgency for me. I sincerely believe that it is a God-ordained civil right for everyone to have the benefit of clean water and of air free of pollutants. Removing the causes of climate change is therefore a moral imperative and must be considered one of the most significant issues of our time.

Climate change is wreaking havoc on the planet. As a pastor, I began to include an ecologically informed exegesis of various texts from scriptures of all faiths that outline or address humankind's responsibility to sustain the environment. I feel strongly that it is imperative for humanity to initiate strategies of collaboration to address climate change—strategies that we used effectively in the Civil Rights Movement. The Civil Rights Movement needed the involvement of everyone who had the courage to stand up for justice and equality. Members of any movement will certainly have differences of opinion, but they share a common goal and are convinced that by working together they can make progress.

In order for the climate change movement to succeed, there must be mutual respect among individuals and groups, and a commitment to each other's well-being. The Civil Rights Movement taught us two words in our search for purpose—*sacrifice* and *risk*. Where there is no commitment to sacrifice and no willingness to risk for the sake of the greater good, there is no courage to accomplish the goals of the cause.

Beginning in 2008, I realized that a part of my purpose was to assist in coordinating religious, business, political, and scientific disciplines so as to create and nurture a more environmentally sensitive citizenry. Collectively we must push our elected representatives to pass legislation that will reduce greenhouse gas (GHG) emissions and fossil fuel consumption worldwide. The Clean Air Act, the Paris Agreement, and the Bonn Meeting all sought to raise awareness regarding the impact of global warming and enact policies to mitigate the effects of climate disruption. Yet, it seems to me that too many political and business leaders continue to oppose these kinds of efforts and deliberately overlook the fact that continuing with business as usual will lead to catastrophe. Around the world many people are aware of the profoundly devastating effects of rising ocean levels, drought, catastrophic storms, and species extinction due to climate disruption. Some feel helpless. Some feel hopeless. Many feel both.

Climate change is complex and daunting, and it takes courage to confront it. We also need to seek and find clear strategies for success. I am inspired by three Rs: Recognize, Refine, and Resolve. I am energized by *recognizing* how much I, and others, have learned so far about climate change. I am intent on *refining* our movement's goals and purpose. And I am *resolved* to pursue these goals. Thus, I am hopeful that my enthusiasm and determination to create a better world will inspire others to join me in taking action. I know from the Civil Rights Movement that it is insufficient merely to espouse political and social rhetoric about the things that need to be addressed. We must also take action. When it comes to climate change, we must not succumb to the lie that this is "fake news." We are already witnessing the consequences of years of disregard for nature, and nature is retaliating in ways that are devastating to the planet's ecosystems and human communities. I am convinced that we must take aggressive action, starting where we are, using what we have, and doing the best that we can while we still have time, so that generations to come will not be doomed by our reckless abandon.

The realities of global warming raise great concern for me. But just as I did with the negative feelings I experienced because of racism, I sustain myself by turning my fears, helplessness, and hopelessness into positive, productive actions. I rely on my God-given powers to listen clearly and then to speak profoundly about this movement.

I challenge you to become an activist right now—unafraid to fight for environmental justice. I hope we all understand that our survival depends on us, working toward the same goal—tackling the factors that cause climate change. I pray as you search for your meaning and purpose that you will have the courage to work toward a sustainable environment.

Chapter Fifteen

Interview with
Rev. Lennox Yearwood Jr.

Margaret Bullitt-Jonas

We interviewed Rev. Lennox Yearwood Jr. on Martin Luther King Jr. Day in 2019, after he attended a signing ceremony for the Clean Energy D.C. Omnibus Act. To date, this is the most aggressive legislation in any state to move to 100 percent renewable energy by 2032—what Rev. Yearwood calls "the epitome of the Green New Deal."[1]

If Dr. King were alive today, what do you think he would say about climate change?
There is no doubt that it would be added to his "isms"—racism, capitalism, militarism. His life ended with him fighting for environmental justice. Today we would see the issues facing the Memphis sanitation workers through the lens of environmental injustice, because they were exposed to toxins they didn't know about. It's worth noting that while many things led to his assassination, he was specifically going to Memphis to fight for the sanitation workers. That was an example of the environmental injustice they were facing at the time.

I have no doubt that from the standpoint of fighting for justice, he would have addressed climate change—that was how his life was trending at the end. He would have definitely taken on the corporate structures of the fossil fuel industry. He would have dealt with the issues of how communities of color in Chicago and the rural communities in Alabama and in North Carolina are placed near fossil fuel production. Sixty-eight percent of people of color live within thirty miles of a coal-fired power plant. He would see that. He would say that climate change is a civil rights issue: that people have a right to clean air and water and the opportunity to thrive on a healthy planet.

The issue of lead poisoning in the water of Flint, Michigan, and the lead paint in Baltimore's low-income housing would be right at the forefront, because he connected the dots so well. That was one of his gifts—to connect the dots in a masterful way.

What led you to include climate as part of your justice ministry?

It was Hurricane Katrina. In 2004, climate justice was part of the framework at Hip Hop Caucus to improve our communities. But it was Katrina that really brought it to the forefront. I'm from Louisiana, and have family and friends in New Orleans. Seeing folks die, and continue to die, because of what happened on August 29, 2005, had a huge impact on me. Also, I got into this work through my dear friend Bill McKibben. I didn't want to come into this movement and be the token black person, so that people would put me in a silo and say, "You're the black person who speaks about environmental justice." I didn't want to be pigeon holed and lose my identity. Having a friend like Bill is an important part of my story: we became best friends around climate; we're connected personally. So I could be "the black reverend guy from Louisiana" and he could be "the tall white guy from Vermont." This is a movement based on friendship and love. And he comes from a place of spirit and faith; we understand that that's a part of who we are.

Bill McKibben is a friend of mine, too, and the first time I saw you was in 2015, when both of you spoke at Harvard Heat Week, an effort to push the university to divest from fossil fuels. Seeing the two of you up on that stage was like watching a living image of the environmental movement and the Civil Rights Movement joining hands in a common effort. How do you connect racial justice and climate change?

Race continues to be a trip wire for the progressive climate movement. Every time race is brought up, we fall over as a movement: we don't deal with that issue. There are a lot of reasons we don't, but if we can just cut that wire, we can move on and get some things done. But as a movement, we're not doing that. Also, we have a siloed, segregated climate movement. We have a movement of those who are fighting for clean water and clean air, and those fighting to stop mountaintop removal. Then there are those who are trying to protect the Arctic and support the indigenous peoples there, the Gwich'in. Still others are fighting to stop pipelines at Standing Rock, and so forth—but even in that part of the movement, there are many different groups and silos. That's one of things we have to find a better way to handle. Our modern movement has been based on certain communities working separately on their own issues, and while there have been many successes, we've tackled issues within a silo.

Now we need a worldwide movement to break down the barriers between all of humanity. That's why today's movement is different from Dr. King's.

His mission was based on equality: how can we make people equal? To-day's movement is not only about equality—it's also about *existence*. If this movement isn't successful, the people on the planet won't exist. Or they will exist in the horrible fashion we're already beginning to see with wars (such as Syria), and with migrants seeking asylum because of droughts and crop failures in Central America.

It's imperative that the climate movement figures out how to get the work done and also mend past wrongs by building bridges across racial, ethnic, and socioeconomic divisions. The movement has to make headway and repair itself at the same time. It's very difficult. It can bring on anxiety, stress, and impatience. The movement wants to progress quickly because of the urgency of the climate crisis; it doesn't have time to bring everybody along—but it *has* to bring everybody along in order to succeed. It has to figure this out: How do we deal with the issue and simultaneously broaden the movement, bringing in new people? This is a challenge that I don't think any movement in history has ever had to deal with. It will take a lot of wisdom, love, faith, and patience to accomplish this.

We also have an enemy that's global. It's not like fighting apartheid in Af-rica. The fossil fuel industry is not only based in more than one country, it's also globally connected throughout systems—financial systems, economic systems, and across every industry. This is no small task.

As people of faith, we believe that this battle is not just ours: it's also the Lord's. We believe that together, we can achieve that. I have seen that. If we can figure these things out, we will be successful. We can cut the trip wire of race. We can get out of the silos. We can become unified. We can share our resources with one another. We can draw on our faith to move forward.

Are you saying that there is a particular role that faith communities can play in this struggle?

Most definitely. Faith is a belief in something outside yourself. It's not all on you. If it's all on you, it can be overwhelming; you can become consumed with anxiety or fear and give up. When you know what we're up against—when you're hearing the reports about what's going on with plastics in the oceans, or extreme wildfires, or what's going on with the Trump administra-tion rolling back basic safeguards to our clean water and air—then you need a faith to believe that there is something out there that will guide you and give you a wisdom to navigate, to do things that make sense. In its larger context, that's what faith can do.

Faith also has a role to play from an institutional standpoint. Men and women who lead faith traditions are important because they have a duty to address injustice. Also, they can provide places to meet and organize, just as they did with the abolitionist movement against slavery, the women's movement, and other movements.

As I said earlier, we are facing a global enemy. But we also have global faith traditions of all kinds, including Hindu, Christian, Muslim, Jewish, Buddhist, and many others. When we pull together, bringing our uniqueness, we are stronger. This is a time when we need faith traditions to share and connect.

Probably the most important thing is to believe that we were made for this moment. We were put on this planet at this time to fight this battle. That's the most amazing gift we've been given by the Almighty: We are so needed. Our people and our gifts were put here at this time for this movement. As overwhelming as the climate crisis may be, we can do this if we all come together.

Christianity has been used to excuse and even to bless injustice of many kinds. Colonialism, slavery, white supremacy, the oppression of Native peoples, and even the assault on the Earth—all of these have been justified on Christian grounds. Obviously, you understand Christianity in a very different way. Would you speak about the ways that being Christian motivates your work for justice?

I earned my Master of Divinity at Howard University, which is where Dr. Howard Thurman taught. He and Dr. Benjamin E. Mays both taught Dr. King. I come out of that tradition. Part of that tradition addresses the question: How do you, as a person of color, deal with Christianity when the very slave boats that brought you to America were named "Jesus"? How do you deal with Christianity when people in the South would go out and lynch somebody and the next day go to church? How do you reconcile that the cross is on the Ku Klux Klan outfits? How do you reconcile, even now, that certain Christians do things that are anti-Muslim or deny climate change? Howard Thurman said, "First and foremost, I'm not a Christian; I'm a follower of Jesus Christ." As a follower of Jesus Christ, I know that he is the God of the oppressed and the disinherited. I take comfort in knowing that the God I serve is the God of the oppressed. He's on the side of those who are victimized. I take comfort throughout His book, the Bible, that He is consistently on the side of the marginalized. I take solace from that: I'm on the right side of God.

Secondly, when I see people who use Christianity in vile ways, this is where love must counter evil. This is where we separate the wheat from the chaff. You can begin to test someone's intentions by asking: When you do those things, where does it come from? Is it coming from a place of love (for God is love) or is it coming from a place within your own culture or tradition that has nothing to do with a God of love? That makes it easy for me to stand up and speak truth to power as a follower of Jesus Christ—and do it with abandon! We go for it, because we have a courage that helps us.

When you get discouraged and feel overwhelmed, where do you turn for strength?

Everybody is different, but I learn from Scripture that the battle is not only mine, but also the Lord's. I am a soldier on this battlefield for justice. I work with young people, and while they don't have the same institutional supports that others had before them, they are very spiritual and connect themselves in different ways. We've lost some, because they commit suicide or get discouraged—it's easy see how that can happen. But I remind them, "This is not your battle alone." You need to fight and to do all you can do, but you have to do this with connection to others and to your faith. You have to believe in something outside yourself. You have to find your anchor. For me, it's God and Christianity, but you've got to find your own anchor. If you don't, you will be blown away. You can't do activism without an anchor. You can't do activism without faith or some form of belief—maybe a belief in the future, or in children. It's great if you have a faith tradition, because there are pieces there that you can hold on to, such as a sacred text, poetry, music—all kinds of things that can inspire you. But you need to have something.

I'm anchored. I'm anchored in my tradition as a person of color, knowing that the people before me had to fight so hard to overcome slavery, to overcome the injustice of Jim Crow, to overcome acts of voter suppression. I'm in a tradition of waking up with those who have already fought. And then, as a person of faith and a minister, I link to this tradition of faith so that whatever I do, my steps are ordered. I know that God is leading me on the right path of fighting for other people, not just for myself. I'm fighting for God's children and for God's planet. That allows me to continue and sometimes to do remarkable things with other people.

Also, I have two children. So I think not only about my own children, but also about other people's children, including the children of people in the fossil fuel industry, and about the world they're going to have around them. We won't be here forever, but the work we do will still be here. The Sunrise Movement helps people know that what we're doing now is laying the groundwork for the next generation.[2] So you can't get discouraged: you're laying the groundwork for the people who come after you.

Who do you count as heroes or role models?

I have so many! I'll name just two. One is Damu Smith (1952–2006), probably the first black climate activist that I saw. At first I was a student activist; then I was a chaplain in the Air Force and thought I was going to go to prison for speaking out against the Iraq war. I saw Damu both at anti-war rallies and at climate rallies. Everyone else at those climate rallies was white. Nobody looked like me! So Damu was important, and his voice was so strong: he had a slot on the local radio station, WPFW, the slot we now have with our show, *Think 100 Percent—The Coolest Show on Climate Change.*

The other person is Dorothy Irene Height (1912–2010), who was in charge of the National Council of Negro Women. She was special because she taught me as a man that there is no movement without women, and that women are powerful. She was in her fifties when she saw the flaws of Dr. King. At the March on Washington, women weren't allowed to speak. Mahalia Jackson sang, but no woman spoke. Even though Height was leading an organization, she didn't speak. She also taught me that you can't do this work if you're jaded or bitter. She said that if you find yourself getting bitter, you have to step away and take time for yourself. People will hurt you in this movement, but if you allow yourself to get bitter, you won't be able to do the work for the people.

What is your theory of social change? On the one hand, you've had dramatic success in inspiring young people, the Hip Hop generation, to register to vote, get to the polls, and engage in the electoral process. On the other hand, you're an activist on the streets: I met you in Washington, D.C., in 2016, when you were about to speak at a Standing Rock rally to protest the Dakota Access Pipeline. What's the dynamic between working inside the halls of Congress and being out on the street? I read a quote in which you said, "The climate movement must be in the streets, suites, and state house (in every state)."[3]

I work with young people, specifically with young people in urban communities, who sometimes don't understand the power they have. My theory of social change is that, if you can get those who feel powerless in this society to feel they have the power from the bottom up, you will create the most change. You can't do this in the spirit of charity, saying: "I'm here to help you; I'm the expert"—but in the spirit of solidarity. This means that if you succeed, I succeed; if I succeed, you succeed. We're clear that we're both in the boat together. If the boat turns over, we both go over. I'm not on the shore, yelling at you; I'm in the boat with you. It means stripping away my degrees, my privilege, anything like that, and doing what Jesus did: we humble ourselves and identify with the powerless.

As we gain power together, as with Hip Hop Caucus, for example, we're going to grow that power together. And when people in our communities see that they have power, change happens: people speak out, come together, and rise up. That's what I've been doing for the past fifteen years. I'm blessed to do this work. It's not easy. People want things to be easier; they want to speak "for" people and be the commentator or translator, but I don't believe that's how it works. Power comes from the people.

If we can get people to rise up, nothing will stop them. People with nothing to lose—like the Dreamers,[4] or the children rising up with Zero Hour,[5] or the Sunrise Movement—feel they have no future. Yet why are they so strong and alive behind their eyes? Because they have nothing to lose. That's what we need to win. We need people who know they have nothing to lose but their chains.

NOTES

1. The Green New Deal is a proposal to address both climate change and income inequality.

2. The Sunrise Movement is a grassroots organization of young people seeking to tackle climate change and create millions of good jobs in the United States through political advocacy.

3. Lennox Yearwood, "Ban Fracking Now!," EcoWatch, March 2, 2017, https://www.ecowatch.com/community/rev_lennox_yearwood_jr.

4. The Dreamers are young immigrants who were brought to the United States without proper documentation. The DREAM Act, which never passed Congress, would have protected them from deportation. "What Is DACA, and Who Are the DREAMers?," Anti-Defamation League, 2019, https://www.adl.org/education/resources/tools-and-strategies/table-talk/what-is-daca-and-who-are-the-dreamers.

5. Zero Hour is a youth-led movement to push for action on climate change and environmental justice. "Getting to the Roots of Climate Change," Zero Hour, http://thisiszerohour.org/.

Chapter Sixteen

Questions to Ponder
and a Spiritual Practice

QUESTIONS TO PONDER

1. All three authors in this section describe their journeys to engage systemic evil and actively work for the rights of oppressed people. When it comes to the climate movement, under what circumstances would you be willing to risk arrest and to carry out an act of nonviolent civil disobedience?

2. If civil disobedience is a new spiritual practice for you, how will you inform yourself about the history, principles, and tactics of nonviolence? Forming an affinity group with people outside of your own socioeconomic sphere, racial/ethnic group, or gender/sexual orientation is often encouraged as part of preparing to carry out civil disobedience. As you form or continue your work with an affinity group, can you name one step you could take to build relationships with people who are different from you?

3. Gerald Durley and Lennox Yearwood Jr. each mention key figures in their own lives and in the larger Civil Rights Movement who taught them and shaped their activism. Peterson Toscano shares inspiring stories of people rising up to claim their humanity and survive oppression. What period of history and which key figures would you like to learn more about? Who are the people in your own family or ancestry that give you courage to endure difficult times and fight for a better future? Who do you count as allies, whether or not they are related to you and whether they are living or dead?

A SPIRITUAL PRACTICE

Rooted and Rising: A Body Prayer

This simple four-part body prayer is adapted from a meditation that Margaret learned from Tilden Edwards many years ago.[1] It expresses both the longing to be centered in the Divine—to live in union with the Holy One who dwells at the center of our being—and the longing to let that love pour out into the world around us. It is based on the natural movement of our bodies: we breathe in, receiving the Divine Mystery who makes a home within us; and we breathe out, encountering the Divine Mystery who makes a home in the world around us, the God of compassion who loves all Creation and who particularly identifies with the powerless and poor.

This meditation can be done indoors or outdoors, alone or with others, and with eyes open or eyes closed.

- Stand upright, as you are able, placing your two feet a comfortable distance apart. If you like, take a few moments to let your body wiggle, stretch, and sway, until you feel relaxed, alert, and ready to begin. Let your knees be soft.
- Feel the good Earth supporting you beneath your feet. Imagine that roots extend from the soles of your feet and stretch down, deep into the Earth.
- Take a few deep breaths, relaxing your belly and your jaw, and feel the air as it fills and empties from your lungs. . . . Then let the breath return to its natural rhythm.

1. Place the palms of your hands together at your heart. This might express your intention to live from your heart: to be mindful, awake, and fully present to each moment.
2. Extend your arms in front of you, making a small bowl or cup with your hands. This might express your desire to offer what you can to the world—to say a kind word, to give a healing touch.
3. Clasp yourself with your arms, crossing your arms over your chest, as if giving yourself a hug. This might express your willingness to receive the love of God, to be fully embraced by God's compassion and peace.
4. Release your arms, extending them in front of you and out to the sides, making a wide semicircle. This might express your desire to love fully and freely, holding nothing back, with the abandon of maple trees releasing their leaves in October. There is no need to hoard divine love, for there is plenty more where that came from!

- Place your palms at your heart and repeat the sequence.

Once you have learned the four gestures, you can coordinate them with the breath: centering your palms at the heart, breathe in; reaching out your hands to form a bowl or cup, breathe out; crossing your arms over your chest, breathe in; opening your arms out wide to the world, breathe out. If you notice that one of the gestures has particular meaning or power for you, you might wish to pause there and let your body experience it for a while, taking in whatever grace or message you receive.

NOTE

1. Rev. Dr. Tilden H. Edwards is an Episcopal priest, retreat leader, author, and founder and senior fellow at Shalem Institute for Spiritual Formation, in Washington, D.C., where he was executive director for more than twenty-seven years. "About Us," Shalem, https://shalem.org/about-us/staff-and-board/.

Section V

ROOTING IN LITURGY, MORAL VISION, AND VOCATION

Section V Introduction

In one way or another, each of the dedicated activists in this book has sunk their spiritual taproot into something enduring that grounds them, like trees extending their roots into deep soil. In this section, John Chryssavgis's reflection on liturgy and theology demonstrates how our deep roots of worship allow us to access the spiritual and religious resources we need for what cultural historian Thomas Berry called the Great Work of our time: to create a life-honoring, Earth-honoring form of society. Then, Cynthia D. Moe-Lobeda's heartfelt letter to her children and grandchildren shows us that these spiritual resources enable us to have moral vision and power for living a life of climate justice. Jim Antal's chapter rounds out this section by urging us to respond to that vision within a vocation of individual and collective action. All three authors remind us that individual changes make a difference, but that because of the scope and speed of the climate crisis, we need more than individual action—we also need systemic change. We need to transform our society and economy at a rate and scope that are historically unprecedented. To do that, we need to use our voices and our votes to make it politically possible to do what is scientifically necessary. This will not be easy. We will have to root ourselves in the love and justice of God.

Chapter Seventeen

The World as Sacrament

Rev. Dr. John Chryssavgis

In recent decades, the world has clearly witnessed alarming ecological degradation, increasing failure to implement environmental policies, and an ever-widening gap between rich and poor. However, during the same period, religious leaders have demonstrated enduring commitment to raising awareness about climate change. Indeed, even before the protection of the environment became "popular" or even "fashionable," Ecumenical Patriarch Bartholomew was dubbed the "green patriarch" by Al Gore and the media for persistently proclaiming the primacy of spiritual values in determining an ecological ethos. I have been privileged to work beside him since he was elected Archbishop of Constantinople and Ecumenical Patriarch in 1991.[1]

With initiatives dating to the early 1980s and the designation of September 1st as a day of prayer for the protection of the planet's natural resources, the call of the Orthodox Church has been followed by member confessions of the World Council of Churches, the Anglican Communion, and, most recently—at the recommendation and with the encouragement of Pope Francis—the worldwide Roman Catholic Church. At the heart of the commitment of the Orthodox Church to Creation care is the conviction that the world is a sacrament—*mysterion* (in Greek)—a mystery revealing the divine in tangible Creation.

Yet the hallmark of these insights and initiatives by the Orthodox Church and its spiritual leader is not in fact success, but humility. Ecumenical Patriarch Bartholomew recognizes that he stands before something greater than any individual—indeed something greater than any church or religion. As he regularly contends, climate change is not primarily a political or a technological issue; it is not essentially a technological or technocratic challenge. It is, as we have come to appreciate, fundamentally a religious and spiritual issue. Religion, therefore, has a vital role to play: after all, a spirituality that remains uninvolved with outward Creation is ultimately uninvolved with the inward mystery too. Thus, although we call this crisis "ecological," which is fair insofar as its results are manifest in the ecological sphere, the crisis is not first of all about ecology. It is a crisis about the way we imagine and treat our planet.

In my own perception of the world and comprehension of Creation care, it took some time to recognize this truth. I had grown up in a religious circle—my father was a parish priest in an Orthodox church—but no one had ever articulated our connection to the Earth that we inhabited. From childhood and throughout my teens, I had participated in liturgical rites that included material and natural elements—bread and wine, oil and wheat, candles and flowers—but no one had ever related them to our everyday living and conduct outside the church setting. In my seminary formation, I had examined the depth of scriptural, sacramental, and spiritual theology—the full range of early and later patristic literature—but no one had defined the broader reach, for instance, of the sacrament of confession from individual immorality to environmental sin.

So I have come to believe that, in our relationship with Creation, we are called to evoke and affirm our interconnectedness with the rest of the world. That is what I would call *the ecumenical imperative of Creation care.* For this sense of interconnectedness reminds us that, in a very distinctive way, the Earth unites us all—before, and beyond, any doctrinal, political, racial, or other differences. We may or may not share religious convictions or ethnic cultures. But we definitely share an experience of the natural environment: we share the air that we breathe, the water that we drink, and the ground that we tread—albeit neither always equally nor always fairly. By some mysterious connection that we do not always understand (and sometimes choose to ignore), the Earth reminds us of our calling to be humble and sensitive. That is arguably our greatest source of hope and joy.

THE DOCTRINE OF DIVINE INCARNATION

For me, in the context of Christian theology and spirituality, the roots of this hope and joy lie in a sacramental consciousness centered on the doctrine of divine incarnation—when God became human with all its historical, spiritual, and cosmic dimensions. Early Christian writers, especially in the East, have normally perceived the incarnation more as a normative movement than as an isolated moment. For instance, Gregory of Nyssa used such terms as "sequence," "consequence," or—in his favorite expression—"progression."[2] That is to say, God always and in all things wills to work the process of divine incarnation. The Word of God assumed flesh two thousand years ago, but that event is only one—even if the most unique and striking—in a series of such incarnations. Self-emptying as divine identification with the world is an essential—not an exceptional—characteristic of God. And if God's presence in the world is not accidental, then neither is the sacredness of Creation coincidental, nor our relationship to the environment incidental.

The only way, then, to relate God to my environment is quite plainly never to separate or alienate Creation from its Creator. For me, this meant I had to turn much of what I had learned on its head, so to speak, in order not so much to change what I believed but rather to discern its wider proportions and cosmic perspectives. And in this theological worldview, Christ stands at the center of the universe, revealing its original beauty and restoring its ultimate destiny. The incarnation is therefore always and properly understood in relation to Creation. In this respect, the Word made flesh is intrinsic to the very act of creation, while historical incarnation is a reaffirmation—not an alteration—of this sacramental reality. This is the understanding of Athanasius of Alexandria, who ascribes cosmological—beyond any purely historical—significance to the incarnation.[3] Similarly, Maximus the Confessor refers to divine *logoi* (principles or seeds) being "conceived" only in the eternal Logos (principle or word) of God: "The divine Word is mysteriously contained in the interior causes (*logoi*) of created beings. . . . The visible conceals the invisible and the tangible reveals the intangible."[4]

THE DIVINE WORD IN THE WORLD

For Gregory Nazianzus, "all things dwell in God alone; all things swarm to him in haste. For God is the end of all things."[5] The ancient Greeks already had a similar worldview, recognizing that *the divine presence is in all things.* Thales exclaimed, "Everything is full of God."[6] And Gregory's contemporary, Basil of Caesarea, claimed that the slightest detail of Creation bore the mark of the Creator:

> Look at a stone, and notice that even a stone carries some mark of the Creator. It is the same with an ant, a bee, a mosquito. The wisdom of the Creator is revealed in the smallest creatures. It is he who has spread out the heavens and stretched out the immensity of the seas. It is he who has also made the tiny hollow shaft of the bee's sting.[7]

The same truth—discovered by science and discerned in theology—is poetically expressed outside of the theological world by the controversial twentieth-century Greek author Nikos Kazantzakis, whose work was banned by the Vatican and condemned by the Church in Greece. Kazantzakis retains a powerful religious worldview of the divine seed in the world—a view that critics might argue is a reinventing of Christianity. For him, created nature is the only premise and promise for either salvation or destruction; it is not a finished product, but a moving ground, an ongoing process of self-transcendence and transformation.

> Everything is an egg, and within it lies the seed of God, restlessly and sleeplessly active. . . . Open your eyes, God is crying; I want to see! Be alert; I want to hear! . . . For to save something [a rock or a seed] is to liberate God within it. . . . Every person has a particular circle of things, of trees, of animals, of people, of ideas—and the aim is to save that circle. . . . The seeds are calling out from inside the earth; God is calling out from inside the seeds. Set God free.[8]

THE MYSTERY OF THE CROSS AND RESURRECTION

However, my theology of the incarnation would remain incomplete if my worldview was not also somehow related to and reflected in the entire "economy" of Christ, which also entails His crucifixion and resurrection. Yet, this, too, was already explicitly articulated in the lives and literature of the Christian classics. Thus, in the mind of the Eastern mystics, everything in Creation is described as undergoing crucifixion in order to achieve resurrection; like the seed in the ground—indeed, like our own selves—everything must die in order to rise. Or, as Maximus the Confessor phrased it, "All phenomena must be crucified."[9] Like Christ, everything sustains incarnation (the tangible nature of materiality), crucifixion (the testing through death in order to be raised to the vertical level of God), and descent into hell (and to the deepest and darkest recesses of the heart), before it can awaken to the light and arise in the life of Christ. It is what Evagrius of Pontus likes to call "a little resurrection" or what John of the Ladder likes to describe as "a resurrection before the Resurrection."

In a conventional—perhaps conservative—Western theological interpretation, the "crucifixion" of nature implies the license to disavow, discard, or even destroy nature with a view to its ultimate resurrection. However, this understanding is not part of the Eastern Christian worldview, which invariably relates the heavenly kingdom to the earthly experience. This is because the "other world" is never disassociated or disconnected from "this world." The way we treat this world determines the way we believe in the "next" life, while the way we profess heaven immediately defines the way we perceive the "present" life. If we contaminate or compromise our environment here and now, then we are insulting and injuring our faith in the hereafter.

The Orthodox liturgical tradition combines this scandal and mystery of the cross with the splendor and majesty of the resurrection—the crucifixion as preparation for the resurrection, and the resurrection as a presupposition of the crucifixion. Together, these two sides of a single reality visualize and materialize the redemption and sanctification of the whole world. Thus, on Good Friday, the Orthodox liturgy sings, "All the trees of the forest rejoice today.

For their nature is sanctified by the body of Christ stretched on the wood [of the cross]." And on Easter Sunday the celebration erupts with elation and effulgence: "Now everything is filled with the light [of the resurrection]: heaven and earth, and all things beneath the earth."[10] Athanasius of Alexandria had already understood this universal dimension: "Christ is the first taste of the resurrection of all . . . the first-fruits of the adoption of all creation . . . the first-born of the whole world in its every aspect."[11]

It is in the resurrection of Jesus Christ, in the abyss of the empty tomb, that the inner meaning of Creation becomes apparent. In a sense, *the original Genesis account of Creation can only be understood in the ultimate light of the resurrection* "that enlightens every person coming into the world" (John 1:9). Through the resurrection, one perceives the end and intent of God for all; one senses in Christ a new creation and a new joy, a new heaven and a new earth. Jesus is recognized as the meaning and life of the whole world, and not simply as a moral redeemer of individual souls. The entire Creation belongs to God; and in God one discovers the true destiny of all Creation. For "he came to what was his own" (John 1:11). He came "to make everyone see what is the plan of the mystery hidden for ages in God, who created all things, so that the wisdom of God in its rich variety might now be made known . . . in accordance with the eternal purpose that God has carried out in Jesus Christ our Lord" (Ephesians 3:9–11).

The two feast days of the early Christian Church that signify new life and new light are Easter and Epiphany; both of these feasts were the principal baptismal days for those wishing to be received into the Church. The Orthodox Church still preserves these powerful images of resurrection and regeneration, and the services for these feasts abound in images that suggest and express the way in which "the entire universe" and "all created matter" contribute to this cosmic liturgy:

> Now everything is filled with light, heaven and earth, and all things beneath the earth; so let all creation celebrate the resurrection of Christ on which it is founded.[12]

> Today creation is illumined; today all things rejoice, everything in heaven and on earth.[13]

> Today the earth and the sea share in the joy of the world.[14]

It is not by chance that both of these central feasts of the Orthodox Church underline the creation of the world "in the first days" (Genesis 1) and understand the significance of the re-creation accomplished "in the latter days" (Hebrews 1:2) in light of the restoration of all things "in the last days" (2 Timothy 3:1).

The promise and pledge of that hope and joy is what instills in me—as in Orthodox believers everywhere—the conviction and commitment to persist in raising awareness about the sacrament of the world. It is what has motivated me to follow the lead of my own church—the Ecumenical Patriarchate and specifically Ecumenical Patriarch Bartholomew, affectionately known over more than two decades as "the green patriarch"—and communicate it to church and parish life, the ecumenical and academic domain, as well as the social and political sector. It has been the foundation and inspiration for my ministry in the Orthodox Church.

NOTES

1. For a selection of Bartholomew's major statements and addresses, see John Chryssavgis, ed., *On Earth as in Heaven: Ecological Vision and Initiatives of Ecumenical Patriarch Bartholomew* (New York: Fordham University Press, 2012). For a summary of Bartholomew's pioneering ecological initiatives, see also John Chryssavgis and Konstantinos Delikostantis, eds., *The Patriarch of Solidarity: Ecological and Global Concerns of Ecumenical Patriarch Bartholomew* (Istanbul: Istos Books, 2013).

2. Gregory of Nyssa, *On the Psalms 3*, in *Patrologia Graeca* (PG), volume 44.441. All translations from classical and patristic sources throughout this chapter are mine.

3. Athanasius of Alexandria, *On the Divine Incarnation*, chapter 17, 45–46.

4. Maximus, *Ambiguum 7* PG 91.1085. See Nicholas Constas, ed., *On the Difficulties in the Church Fathers: The Ambigua*, vol. 1 (Cambridge, MA: Harvard University Press, 2014), 75–141.

5. Gregory Nazianzus, *Dogmatic Poems 29*, in PG 37.508.

6. Thales, *Fragment 22*.

7. Basil of Caesarea, *Commentary on Psalm 32*, 3 in PG 29.329.

8. Nikos Kazantzakis, *Askitiki: Salvatores Dei*, 5th ed. (Athens: no publisher, 1979), 85–89. Translation mine from the original Greek.

9. Maximus the Confessor, *Theological Chapters* 67 PG 90.1108B.

10. Translation of the last two quotations are mine. For the Orthodox paschal service, see Mother Mary and Kallistos Ware, *The Lenten Triodion* (South Canaan, PA: St. Tikhon's Seminary Press, 2001).

11. Athanasius of Alexandria, *On the Divine Incarnation*, chapter 20 (48–49), and *Against the Arians* II, 64 PG 26.281–84.

12. Paschal Canon, 3rd Ode.

13. Epiphany, *Sticheron* (January 6).

14. Prayer, "Great Blessing of the Waters," January 6. My translation. For an alternative translation of this prayer, see Mother Mary and Kallistos Ware, *The Festal Menaion* (South Canaan, PA: St. Tikhon's Seminary Press, 1998), 356–57.

Chapter Eighteen

A Letter

Cynthia D. Moe-Lobeda, PhD

To my precious children and grandchildren:

I long to leave you a world of beauty and goodness, of laughter and love. And indeed, these will never die. Yet I will also leave you a world of disaster at a scale unknown to any of the humans who preceded us.

I would give my life to reverse the runaway climate crisis that we bequeath unwittingly to you and your friends. You will face a reality that seems to defy the human capacity for survival and flourishing: the climate catastrophe into which previous generations—including my own—have hurled you. However, I do believe with the core of my being that the great Mystery whom Christian traditions call God will redeem this good Creation and bring it into fullness of life for all, despite the raging fury of climate change. God will use human beings and other creatures and elements of the Earth community in that saving work.

I know, too, that a disempowering paradox haunts the quest for hope and for moral and spiritual power in the face of climate catastrophe and the worldwide economic system that fuels it. On the one hand, we cannot meet the challenge of climate change unless we face very clearly and honestly the magnitude of what is going on. For high-consuming people, this includes confronting the tormenting reality that we have played a role in causing global warming. Yet on the other hand, the more we recognize this reality, the more powerless we may feel. Ironically, the knowledge necessary for taking moral action can also impede it.

What then are we to do? How are we to gain and maintain the fortitude to see clearly what is going on, while also maintaining hope and a steadfast commitment to act in the deep and radical ways necessary to mitigate the worst effects of climate change? Where will your generations and mine find the wisdom, courage, and hope to face what seems so impossible to face, and

117

to choose life in the midst of this human-caused calamity? How will the Great Spirit cultivate these gifts in us?

Perhaps a few clues from my story may provide small seeds of hope, wisdom, and moral-spiritual power for you and your allies. With that hope in mind, here is part of my tale.

TWO LIFE-CHANGING EXPERIENCES

When I was a very young woman, I fell into deep despair about the insidious power of systemic injustice and my own part in it. I had begun to learn that vast and powerful economic systems structured life in such a way that people like me (citizens of the United States who were white and economically privileged) could consume exorbitantly while others were exploited, impoverished, or even destroyed by those very systems. After a few years of fervent efforts to "make a difference" through activism, I fell into a desolate world of guilt and hopelessness. It could have cost me my life.

Two things happened to rescue me from that state. In these two interactions, the Spirit re-kindled a spark of hope and self-love in me. First, something moved me to seek out a former church youth group leader for help. When I knocked on the door of his dental office, he saw my face, closed the office, walked me outside to a creek in the woods, opened his Bible, and read to me from Romans. Suddenly I was engulfed by an utterly overwhelming and stunningly real sense of God's limitless and unconditional love for me. I knew that I would be embraced by that love for all time, regardless of what I did or did not do. I will never forget that truth, and the feeling of extraordinary peace that accompanied it. Even more, I realized that just as I am beloved beyond measure, so, too, is every person who walks the Earth.

The second experience came when I sought out someone who was deeply aware of the iron clasp of systemic sin on U.S. society, but who nevertheless maintained active hope and joy. I was led to confide in a Lutheran pastor, a leader in the anti-nuclear movement and in other streams of social justice work. Confessing to him my despair, I puzzled, "Knowing what you know, John, how is it that you can have hope for this world?" I will never forget his response. "Cindy," he said, "I know the end of the story." By this he meant that the power of God to liberate Creation is stronger than anything else and will prevail. Devastation is not the last word. In some way that we do not grasp, the last word is life raised up out of death. We have heard the end of the story. In the midst of suffering and death—be it individual, social, or ecological—the promise given to the Earth community is that abundant life in God will reign. So speaks the resurrection.

In all honesty, I do not know what this promise means for us and for Earth's community of life. It does *not* lessen our call to build a more just, compassionate, and sustainable world; it does *not,* that is, allow us to sit back and succumb to magical thinking that God will do all the work. That notion is absurd, because God works through human beings. Nor does resurrection hope ensure our survival as a species in the face of climate change. It *does* ensure that the radiant Good at the center of reality ultimately will bring fullness of life. We are to live trusting in that promise. This resurrection promise is a profound source of hope.

GUIDING PRACTICES

These two touchstone experiences are wellsprings from which I drink hope in the face of climate reality. Over the years, they have suggested to me a number of guiding practices that help me maintain hope and a sense of power to make a difference. Here are two: practicing "critical mystical vision" and practicing paradox.

Practicing Critical Mystical Vision

I have long taught that moral vision entails seeing three things at once. The first is seeing "what is going on," especially by recognizing the magnitude of structural evil entwined in our lives. What do I mean? Well, neither you nor I nor most of the people in our circles want to hurt others. In fact, we hunger to make a difference for the good in people's lives! That is how you, dear grandchildren, are being raised, as were your parents, grandparents, great-grandparents, and beyond. Nevertheless, our relationships with others near and far are shaped—by economic, political, cultural, and military systems—into patterns that require economic and racial exploitation and that generate ecological disaster, including climate change.

To illustrate, while the world's small minority of high-consuming people (including everyday middle-class citizens of the United States like us) bear most of the responsibility for the climate crisis, those least responsible for it are suffering and dying, first and foremost, from it. I find this injustice haunting, especially its race and class dimensions. By this I mean that climate change is wreaking death and destruction especially on impoverished people who also are disproportionately people of color. Island people forced from their lands by rising sea levels, subsistence farmers whose crops are lost to climate change, and many coastal people without resources to protect against and recover from the fury of climate-related weather disaster are not the people largely responsible for greenhouse gas emissions.[1] Nor are they, for the most part, white. Friends in India taught me to think of this as "climate colonialism."[2]

Seeing "what is going on," in this sense, requires moral courage. You may find yourself feeling devastated by Earth's demise and by the profound human suffering around you. So you'll need a second form of vision: seeing "what could and should be." By this I mean envisioning ways of living and structuring our society that are socially just and ecologically sound. This is the blessed vision of hope that breaks through the wasteland of social and ecological violence. Hope springs forth from the courage, tenacity, and creativity of people and movements in our own land and around the globe who are generating more ecologically sane and economically equitable practices, policies, institutions, lifestyles, and worldviews. Thank God, these movements are erupting everywhere, including in your own homes and churches, dear ones!

The third lens is seeing that we human creatures are not alone in the quest for more just and sustainable ways of living. God—the life-giving, life-saving Source of the cosmos—is with and within Earth's elements and creatures (we humans included), luring Creation toward God's intent that all may have life and have it abundantly (John 10:10). May you remember each day that this Spirit enables life and love to reign over death and destruction, even when that seems impossible and quite the opposite appears to be true.

Recently, my understanding of moral vision has expanded to include a fourth lens. It is the lens that always sees the astounding goodness, sensual beauty, and infinite meaning of life here in Garden Earth. This lens recognizes that Earth is meant to be a paradise for its creatures to relish with all of our senses. Do remember, even in bleak times, to savor the goodness and sensual beauty that surrounds us! Let it nourish your experience of meaning, joy, self-respect, and love. We are never bereft of beauty or goodness, if only we recognize it—the glorious sky or the touch of air on skin, a twinkling leaf in the wind or the sound of song, the color purple next to blue or the kindness of a stranger.

I believe that by using these four lenses, you will discover your moral power for living toward climate justice. Please understand that vision of this sort is subversive, for it reveals a future in the making and breeds hope for moving into it. I have a hunch that if you practice this four-fold vision, you will receive and embody the Spirit's life-giving power. This is the power to recognize and resist worldviews, power arrangements, policies, and practices that perpetuate our current mad orgy of consumption and the corporate-and-finance-driven, fossil-fueled, global economy that requires and enables that consumption. And it is the power to forge more just, sustainable, and life-supporting alternatives. This power is the Spirit of the living God, shaping us to love neighbor as self and to serve and preserve Garden Earth.

Practicing Paradox

Human beings are master liars, particularly adept at lying to self. Lying is deadly. So, too, is numbness, the refusal to feel—especially to feel anger and painful emotions. Lying and running from feeling throw poison on the green plant of human spirit. I learned early to drink these poisons. I recall my decision as a girl, for example, never to be angry because—I had come to believe—anger is a vice. I ran from feeling my anger. So, too, I fled emotional pain, whispering unconsciously to myself, "Feeling is too painful; I will sidestep it." I lied to myself about despair because Christians—I thought—do not despair.

Now, I know better. Telling the truth to yourself and feeling fully—including anger and painful emotions—are utterly essential to wholeness of being and fullness of power for the good. Truth-telling and honestly feeling require accepting paradox. Hope is born for me as I learn to accept and even welcome the vivid paradox in which human life—including my life—unfolds. In particular I mean this:

- *Knowing both hope and despair*. The key is to say, "Yes, I do have both hope and despair, *and*, because I put my trust in the justice-seeking love of God, my hope prevails.
- *Beauty and brutality entwined in human life*. This paradox of the human species stuns. Capable of beauty, creativity, and goodness beyond imagining, we also engender brutality unspeakable. The same species that creates music to heal the soul, willingly risks life to save others, spins pure joy through laughter and love, and engenders so much that is good and beautiful is now brutally destroying the delicate conditions necessary for life as we know it to continue on Earth.
- *Joy and sorrow coexisting*. Silenced sorrow eats one alive. So I am learning to experience the sorrow that wells within me, while knowing that it is survivable and need not wipe out my joy. Joy can spring forth even while sorrow remains, joy in the most beautiful and simple gifts of being alive—a welcoming smile, a gentle touch on an aching back, the beauty of sky, the glorious melody of birdsong.

CLOSING

And so, my cherished children and grandchildren, my heart longs to protect you from the horrors of a world assaulted by raging climate catastrophe. But I cannot. Still I pray that you may know that the God of justice-seeking, Earth-relishing love will never cease to embrace you and your world! For "neither death, nor life, nor angels, nor rulers, nor things present, nor things to come, nor powers, nor height, nor depth, nor anything else in all creation, will be able to separate us from the love of God in Christ Jesus" (Romans 8:38–39). May you trust that the Spirit will cultivate in you the hope and moral courage that you need to heed the God of life despite all that befalls, always knowing that your failures and shortcomings (and there will be many) are forgiven. The intimate Mystery we call God will nourish hope, joy, and moral-spiritual power. Together with others around the globe, we will continue to build a world in which Earth's community of life can flourish with justice and joy.

NOTES

1. As recognized by the U.N. Conference on Sustainable Development, climate change "represents the gravest of threats to the survival" of some island nations. See "Future We Want: Outcome Document," Sustainable Development: Knowledge Platform, July 27, 2012, http://sustainabledevelopment.un.org/futurewewant.html.

2. Some time ago, I was invited to India to work with church and seminary leaders on matters of eco-justice. They gently taught me to re-see climate change as climate colonialism. "Climate change," declared a high-level Indian church leader, "is caused by the colonization of the atmospheric commons. . . . [T]he powerful nations and the powerful within [them] . . . have emitted and continue to emit greenhouse gases beyond the capacity of the planet to withstand. However the . . . communities with almost zero footprint . . . bear the brunt of the consequences."

Chapter Nineteen

Fighting Climate Change

Our Responsibility, Our Vocation, Our Salvation

Rev. Dr. Jim Antal

"An opportunity for which the Church was born." How many churchgoers view climate change like that? At least one does. His name is Bill McKibben, the writer and environmental activist who co-founded the global climate action group 350.org. This was how he described the challenge of the climate crisis in 2006.

But when the United Nations's Intergovernmental Panel on Climate Change (IPCC) released its 2018 report, it didn't quite sound like an opportunity for the Church.[1] The report detailed the impacts of warming the planet by 1.5°C—a temperature rise that is already "baked in." The scientists who authored the report said that the world must quickly undertake "rapid and far-reaching" changes on an "unprecedented" scale to reduce emissions over the next decade in order to avoid the worst impacts of climate change. Scientists declared that avoiding catastrophe will require transforming the world economy at a speed and scale that has "no documented historic precedent." The report was frightening and overwhelming.

Yet "Good News" was proclaimed. It came not from the Church, but in a *New York Times* op-ed piece. The headline was striking: "Stopping Climate Change Is Hopeless. Let's Do It." After enumerating many of the most depressing realities of climate change, the authors, Auden Schendler and Andrew P. Jones, declared, "We're perfect for the job. If the human species specializes in one thing, it's taking on the impossible. We are constitutionally equipped to understand this situation." Schendler and Jones lifted up the power of spiritual practice and briefly named some of the current habits we must exchange for new practices and disciplines that have the power to be salvific (my word). They believe that the path out of this mess will lead us to become more like a "beloved community."

123

The work [that is required of us] would endow our lives with some of the old-est and most numinous aspirations of humankind: leading a good life; treating our neighbors well; imbuing our short existence with timeless ideas like grace, dignity, respect, tolerance and love. The climate struggle embodies the essence of what it means to be human, which is that we strive for the divine.[2]

To become fully human in the way Schendler and Jones describe, humanity needs to pivot on a scale and with the same urgency that the Allies mustered in response to World War II. Many essays have made this point and several organizations are based on it.[3] There's a reason why those who rose to the challenge of resisting Hitler came to be known as "the greatest generation." More than 50,000,000 individuals sacrificed their lives to defeat a terrible threat. The tens of thousands of churches that converted their pristine lawns to victory gardens, and the tens of millions of Americans who became vegetarians also made radical changes to protect freedom and peace.

Between 1941 and 1945, with civilization in the balance, hundreds of millions of people accepted the reality that "we don't get to do what we want. We have to do what needs to be done." Not only did this make their generation great, but many also found this reorientation personally fulfilling. It gave deep meaning to many lives.

Over the past fifteen years, I've been blessed to know and love hundreds of people—old and young, secular and religious—who have devoted their lives to what must be done to avert climate catastrophe and who have discovered deep joy in doing so. Now, more than fifty years after the first report on climate change was delivered to President Johnson, many people are beginning to acknowledge that climate change represents an existential threat to humanity—and not just to humanity, but also to all of Creation. We are in the midst of the sixth extinction. The continuity of life itself is now in jeopardy.

The lives of millions of people worldwide have already been upended, never to return to what they had been, never to unfold in their hoped-for ways. The charred wildfire ashes in California that were once homes and then were washed away by an unprecedented torrent of rain and a deluge of mud are but one example. More than five million Syrian refugees fleeing drought, famine, and civil war is another.[4]

I'm reminded of one of the postcards created by the group Artists Against Nuclear War. It portrayed a father from the 1950s standing tall and proud with his arm on his son's shoulder, saying to his son, "All of this can be yours," as they look out on missiles of mass destruction, stealth bombers, and a nuclear mushroom cloud in the background.

We must not go down in history as the generation that turns over to our children a devastated planet. And we don't have to: a different response is already emerging. Americans are now beginning to grasp the fact that climate change is happening. It's human caused and it already poses a threat to the very existence of life as humans have always known it. Many people are raising fundamental and profound questions: Should we bring children into the world we have created? Should we move to a safer location, less likely to be inundated by rising seas or less prone to fire? These are some of the ways the existential threat impacts personal choice and aspiration.

But what if, in facing the threat that climate change presents to our personal hopes and dreams, we generated another change—a change in the human prospect as fundamental and as universal as climate change? What if, by fully accepting that the activities of seven generations of humans have wrecked our common home, we became free to embrace a fresh understanding of human fulfillment and *vocation*?

The traditional understanding of "vocation" is best expressed by Frederick Buechner's oft-quoted formulation: "The place God calls you to is the place where your deep gladness and the world's deep hunger meet."[5] While important and beautifully stated, this description focuses on individual vocation and personal gladness. But living as we are in the "days of Noah,"[6] our vocation must be communal as well as personal. And our vocation in these modern days "before the flood" is not determined by what makes each of us "glad." The crisis we face places an inescapable moral claim on our generation, and therefore on each of us. We must do what urgently needs to be done, using the unique gifts each of us brings. As we live into this new vocation, we will discover blessings much deeper than personal gladness. Working together on behalf of Creation, we will, as C. S. Lewis named it, be "surprised by joy."[7]

It's up to those of us alive in this precious moment, this unprecedented crossroads, amid this unconscionable vulnerability, to change what appears to be inevitable. While physics and chemistry are telling us that the arc of the universe is bending toward extinction, our generation still has the power to bend the moral arc of the universe toward justice (as Rev. Dr. Martin Luther King Jr. described it) as we revive Creation.

Imagine if each of us began to embrace this new understanding of vocation. Imagine if our generation stepped up to the fact that it's truly up to us. Like the Greatest Generation, can we set aside our personal aspirations in order to address the greatest threat humanity has ever faced?

Let's be clear—this calling will ask much of us, including sacrifice. But dedication to a larger cause often comes with surprises. For example, after being arrested for engaging in nonviolent civil disobedience around environmental issues, I was surprised, during the hours and days that I spent in jail, to experience the deepest sense of freedom I have ever known.

Faith communities have a crucial role to play. In my book *Climate Church, Climate World*, I ask what it would be like if clergy were to give at least as much attention to *collective* salvation in their sermons as they now give to *personal* salvation.[8] On many occasions, I have challenged congregations whose understanding of mission has become excessively self-focused to realize that, like all houses of worship, they are not called to be a church for themselves. They are called to be "a church for others." Just as the Apostle Paul tells us that Jesus "poured himself out for others" (Philippians 2:7), so our generation must now pour ourselves out for others—including for generations yet to come.

What if every religious leader, inspired by Pope Francis's encyclical, *Laudato Si'*,[9] made this declaration to their congregation: "Because we are living on the hinge of history, I need to devote 25 percent of my leadership to combat climate change." What if university presidents formed a coalition to commit at least 25 percent of their curriculum to amplifying their students' understanding of climate change and their vocational commitment to restoring Creation? What if seminaries, together with all institutions where clergy are trained, acknowledged that the continuity of Creation has been broken, and that humanity is now unified by the challenge of climate change? What if we all were to recognize that on this new Eaarth[10] (to borrow from Bill McKibben), the role of each and every faith practice is to inspire people of faith to dedicate their lives to restoring Creation?[11]

It's time to reread Scripture and embrace the theme that is everywhere apparent: God calls communities, not just individuals! If we collapse the notion of vocation into the narrow confines of a single life, or a single lifetime, we're ignoring a major thrust of Scripture.

Humanity itself now has a vocation. Yes—each of us must continue to develop our personal gifts and hold on to our personal aspirations. But we must do so in response to our common calling to counter the climate crisis. We can and must create a social climate in which each person's gifts and passions are celebrated insofar as they help heal Creation and build a more just, sustainable society.

This, of course, flies in the face of the capitalist aspirations that have dominated America for well over a century. If we are to meet the challenge of climate change, we must exchange the dominant ethos of individualism for a recognition that we're all in this together. In place of the American dream of consumption, we must rediscover the beauty, diversity, and healing qualities of the natural world. We must learn that meaning and joy derive less from self-interest, status, and prestige and more from equality, community, vulnerability, and empathy.

If we are to navigate this transition, we must allow ourselves to grieve in at least two ways. First, we must mourn the loss of the future that we dreamed of for our children. As with so many profound transitions, only by grieving will we, as a society, be freed to accept the moral and economic transformation that we need to make. Religious leaders must move to the front lines as facilitators of this process.

Second, we must face our generation's delayed action on climate change with searing honesty and truth telling, and then grieve the devastation and wreckage that could have been avoided. Not only does this grieving lead to self-examination and personal change, it also prompts us to hold fossil fuel corporations accountable for privileging profit while ravaging the Earth. And just as important, this grieving connects us with the poor, the marginalized, and people of color, who are hit first and worst.

Religious leaders must create enough moral space in our collective life to make such grief and accountability normative. In this way, instead of being paralyzed, congregations can be empowered to embrace the activities in which front-line congregations are already engaging, such as divesting from fossil fuel stocks; installing solar panels; inviting weekly testimony detailing acts of witnessing to climate justice; signing, collecting, and blessing pledge cards to vote on climate in upcoming elections; hosting truth and reconciliation conversations on climate change; and preaching regularly on intergenerational responsibility.

Our generation's window of opportunity is not yet shut. Climate scientists have done their part. They will forever be recognized as heroes by our progeny. And the engineers have done their part. The cost of solar power is less than 1/200th of what it was when President Carter first put solar panels on the roof of the White House. The researchers have done their part. Professor Mark Jacobson at Stanford has shown that using today's technology, virtually every country in the world can transition to 100 percent renewable energy by 2050.

More and more people are now readily saying, "I want to help. I want to do something." Just as activists and political leaders are raising the prospect of a Green New Deal, it's time for religious leaders to remind people the world over of the "Original Green New Deal"—God's great gift of Creation.[12]

What would it be like to be a member of the generation that (finally!) blew the whistle and declared, "Not on my watch!"? It would involve relinquishing much of what we currently pursue in our quest for happiness and accepting that consumerism and selfishness will never satisfy our deepest longings. In subordinating our personal aspirations so that we can devote our lives to a larger calling, we may begin to understand Jesus's insight that those who lose their life will find it.

Such devotion will create an unstoppable mandate to restore Creation. As we work to care for each other and all Creation, a new experience of freedom and joy will emerge. Humanity must seize the opportunity to become true protectors of God's good Earth. This is an opportunity for which the Church—and all of humanity—were born. Let's do it!

NOTES

1. Intergovernmental Panel on Climate Change, *Global Warming of 1.5° C: An IPCC Special Report*, Intergovernmental Panel on Climate Change, 2018, https://report.ipcc.ch/sr15/pdf/sr15_spm_final.pdf.

2. Auden Schendler and Andrew P. Jones, "Stopping Climate Change Is Hopeless. Let's Do It," *New York Times*, October 6, 2018, https://www.nytimes.com/2018/10/06/opinion/sunday/climate-change-global-warming.html.

3. For example: Bill McKibben, "We're Under Attack from Climate Change—and Our Only Hope Is to Mobilize Like We Did in WWII," *The New Republic*, August 15, 2016, https://newrepublic.com/article/135684/declare-war-climate-change-mobilize-wwii; The Climate Mobilization website, https://www.theclimatemobilization.org/; Paul Gilding, *The Great Disruption* (New York: Bloomsbury, 2012); Paul Gilding, "The Earth Is Full," filmed February 2012, TED video, 16:25, https://www.ted.com/talks/paul_gilding_the_earth_is_full.

4. Matthew Taylor, "Climate Change 'Will Create World's Biggest Refugee Crisis,'" *The Guardian*, November 2, 2017, https://www.theguardian.com/environment/2017/nov/02/climate-change-will-create-worlds-biggest-refugee-crisis.

5. Frederick Buechner, *Wishful Thinking—A Seeker's ABC* (New York: Harper-One, 1992).

6. Matthew 24:37; Luke 17:26. See also Dale Aukerman, "As in the Days of Noah," in *Darkening Valley: A Biblical Perspective on Nuclear War* (Harrisonburg, VA: Herald Press, 1989).

7. C. S. Lewis, *Surprised by Joy: The Shape of My Early Life*, rev. ed. (Houghton Mifflin Harcourt, 1995).

8. Jim Antal, *Climate Church, Climate World: How People of Faith Must Work for Change* (Lanham, MD: Rowman & Littlefield, 2018).

9. [Pope] Francis, *Laudato Si'—Praise Be to You: On Care for Our Common Home* (Vatican: Libreria Editrice Vaticana, 2015).

10. See Bill McKibben, *Eaarth: Making a Life on a Tough New Planet* (New York: Times Books, 2010).

11. McKibben, *Eaarth*.

12. Jim Antal, "America Needs a Green New Deal to Create Infrastructure, Jobs and a Just Economy," *Des Moines Register*, January 24, 2019, https://www.desmoinesregister.com/story/opinion/columnists/2019/01/24/column-america-needs-green-new-deal-create-jobs-just-economy-clean-energy-climate-change-religion/2663471002/.

Chapter Twenty

Questions to Ponder
and a Spiritual Practice

QUESTIONS TO PONDER

1. John Chryssavgis details the rich liturgical history that supports a ministry of Creation care within Orthodox Christianity. If you are a person of faith, what are the sacred writings, teachings, and worship traditions that connect you with God's Creation? What are the readings and rituals in your religious tradition that have taken on fresh meaning and power in the context of climate crisis? If you are not part of a faith tradition, what are rituals that instill in you a sense of the sacredness in nature and a feeling of humility and interconnectedness with all that lives?

2. Cynthia Moe-Lobeda's letter to her children and grandchildren expresses her great sorrow about the world she is passing on to them, but also urges them to practice "critical mystical vision" in order to develop the courage and compassion that will be needed in the days ahead. If you could write a letter to your children (or other young people in your life) about the climate crisis we are facing now and that they will endure in the future, what would you say? What words of lament *and* encouragement would you share with them?

3. In his chapter, Jim Antal asks, "What if every religious leader, inspired by Pope Francis's encyclical, *Laudato Si'*, made this declaration to their congregation: 'Because we are living on the hinge of history, I need to devote 25 percent of my leadership to combat climate change.'" If you are a religious leader, what would such a commitment look like for you? If you are a member of a congregation, what would it look like for your house of worship to devote 25 percent of its time and resources to address climate change? What percentage of your own life would you say is dedicated to the cause of climate justice? What steps can you take to increase that percentage?

A SPIRITUAL PRACTICE

Practicing Gratitude

When we feel frightened, lonely, or resentful, practicing gratitude can help us remember the underlying blessings of our lives—including the gift of life itself. Gratitude can renew our sense of wonder and awe. It has a mysterious ability to reconnect us with God and restore inner peace. As Joanna Macy and Chris Johnstone point out, gratitude builds trust and generosity, serves as an antidote to consumerism, and motivates us to act for our world.[1]

The practices below can be tried out at different times.

- Go outside for a walk and receive every experience as a gift—the sight of the sky, the feel of your foot on the ground, the crack in the sidewalk, the girl walking her dog, the call of a crow. Walk slowly. Everything you see, hear, smell, and touch is a gift. It is surprising that anything is here at all! Notice something you have never noticed before. Who is the One who created all this? Who is the One who is with you as you walk? Give thanks.
- Take a sheet of paper and imagine that it portrays your grateful heart. What is in it? Make a drawing or write down what you are thankful for.
- Look back over the day. Look back over the year. Look back over your life. Notice the gifts. If you like, make a list.
- Sitting in silence, breathe with awareness. This breath is a gift. This moment is a gift. This heartbeat is a gift. Death could come at any moment, yet here you are, alive! All is a gift. Be thankful.

NOTE

1. Joanna Macy and Chris Johnstone, *Active Hope: How to Face the Mess We're in without Going Crazy* (Novato, CA: New World Library, 2012), 43–56.

Section VI

UPROOTED, REPLANTED, AND RISING

Section VI Introduction

This section contains hard truths and holds us accountable in searing, yet necessary, ways. All three authors speak of the experience of being "uprooted." Kiran Oommen is the youngest of our contributors and writes about his journey away from the church in his climate activism—while retaining some key principles from his religious upbringing. Tink Tinker speaks about the American Indian experience of being violently uprooted from the very land that sustained their people for thousands of years. His postcolonial critique of Christianity is honest, raw, and humbling. Tim DeChristopher's chapter reflects on what it means to be uprooted from the gods we must leave behind as we face the massive upheaval of climate disruption and begin to learn new ways of being. All three authors hold us accountable both to our past sins and idolatry and to the young people and future generations who are dealing with the fallout of those sins.

Chapter Twenty-One

The People around Me

Reflections from a Post-Christian Anarchist

Kiran Oommen

When I was in college, I took a theology class from a professor who was not only a radical theologian but also a veteran of the anti-nuke movement. Despite his obvious passion for the world, he claimed he felt burned out. According to him, the anti-nuke movement failed because they didn't achieve their goals—ending the production and possession of nuclear armaments. After seeing so many of his peers "grow up," lose their interests in political change, and become the apathetic middle class they had once rejected, my professor had a pessimistic outlook on change. In a class discussion, I professed to being a staunch existentialist. My professor, knowing of my work in the environmental movement, stopped me to ask what I meant by that. He assumed that I saw a "greater good" to my work and was confused as to why I dedicated so much time and energy to something if I didn't see an ultimate purpose to it.

But here's the thing, I told him. I don't think I will save anything. Call me a pessimist, but I think we just might lose. Climate change is happening right now, and the current power structures give little to no opportunity to address it effectively. And yet—those realities are irrelevant to why I'm fighting. I don't know if there's a God out there; I don't know if there's a greater good; I don't know if there is a knowable Truth. I don't even know if my life has a purpose. But there are two things I do recognize: I have an intrinsic need to *find* purpose, and that is essentially tied up in community. I'm not here to win, I'm here to fight.

He paused, and then responded, "I wish I'd had your perspective when I was your age. I don't think I would have burned out."

I don't want to claim that my perspective is "better" than any others; I don't think it is. However, it's crucial for me to be honest because I think we need a diversity of activist philosophies if we are going to get a diversity of activists. And that's why a twenty-one-year-old anarchist punk is writing in an anthology of religious environmental activists. I may not have found God, but I did find church. Do I go to church? Not anymore; the music was too slow, and I couldn't find enough wine. However, what I found growing up as a preacher's kid in the United Church of Christ (UCC) was the value of having a passionate, organizing community. Once I realized that, I knew I could never do without it.

When I moved to Seattle for college, I began my search for this organizing community. Initially, that group included my peers. The first thing I noticed when I started organizing with students was that people liked to share their first protest stories. Everyone remembered their first march, or that radical-izing professor who inspired them to get out on the streets, or the moment when they realized the vastness of social issues that persist on a daily basis. Nearly everyone, that is, except me. Growing up in the activist community of the UCC in Eugene, Oregon, I'd always considered organizing basic to my way of life. There was never even a question of whether or not to be a part of a social movement, because that was a necessary part of my community. The question *I* had faced instead as I entered my teens was what social movements I wanted to be a part of. I remember a middle school Halloween dance where I dressed up as "global warming." I had decided climate change was the most all-encompassing issue—and definitely the scariest. Hence perfect material for a Halloween costume, right? Apparently not. Not only did everyone ask me what my costume was, nobody got my point. (A classmate who didn't consider the paper graph that was safety-pinned to my baggy, black shirt very flattering sniggered and asked me, "Don't you want to get laid?" I wasn't too put off, though; I didn't know what that meant.)

You might be wondering what social movements I decided on. My first ac-tivist group outside of the religious community was the Cascadia Forest De-fenders, a radical environmentalist direct-action group I joined in high school. Not long after I started working with them, I was asked if I wanted to sign on as a co-plaintiff on *Juliana v. United States of America*, the federal climate change lawsuit represented by the law nonprofit Our Children's Trust. In the spring of my senior year of high school I got an e-mail from an old friend who was already a plaintiff on the case: "I know you've been organizing around climate change issues; would you like to sue the government?"

What a strange idea, I thought, but why not? I'm part of twenty-one youth plaintiffs on the case, and our argument is that the federal government's actions to support the fossil fuel industry and aggravate climate change violate our constitutional rights to life, liberty, and property. We aren't asking for compen-sation, but, rather, a court order for a science-based climate-recovery plan. This means integrating the climate science that seeks to set us on track to mitigate climate change and stabilize the planet's atmosphere into actual climate policy. This should be an obvious step, but unfortunately the United States has refused to consider such a massive system overhaul. Also, our success as plaintiffs would mean asserting a stable climate system as a constitutional right, setting the stage to justify all sorts of other actions against the exploitation of the Earth. Our group has already passed numerous hurdles. We are currently fighting for our right to go to trial. We don't know what the outcome will be, but so far, we have been successful. This "strange idea" I signed on to three years ago is not so strange anymore. Between our attorneys representing us in the courts and the mass mobilization of organizers all around the country, the government cannot ignore us as they originally thought they could.

We are giving climate change our best shot, but I still haven't been able to convince myself that the struggles we face will be solved. Discovering a philosophy behind my activism has been a journey of learning to live with the fact that our work may never stop the damage of climate change. Through environmental organizing, I am working every day toward a more purposeful life. I work with brilliant people who continue to dedicate their lives to finding new and innovative ways to challenge the powers that be. I truly believe this is our only chance. Because of my experience growing up in the UCC, I learned not only to appreciate but also to *need* intentional communities of passion to give life the meaning I search for. That's why I continue to work with this group.

If I have any hope, it's because of people. Post high school, I've been involved in numerous activist groups in the Pacific Northwest, mostly focusing on climate issues but also on whatever seems pressing at a given time. This means I've found myself protesting everything from gentrification to white nationalism. The work we do is always centered around the issues, but the communities we create while fighting are what keep me going. And these communities are so much wider than the city I live in. As a child, family vacations almost always involved my parents wanting to visit a local church. I used to think that perhaps they just loved churches. However, as I began to discover my own community, I realized that it was more than that. When I go to new places, I go to punk shows. They may be dirty, hard to find, and certainly not recommended as tourist destinations, but no matter where I am in the world, I know I can find passionate community in those spaces. If you substitute graffitied basements, cheap beer, and punk rock for stained glass sanctuaries, coffee, and hymns, you can see how much I take after my parents.

I spent a term studying in Sweden, and the first week I was there I found a punk show. The friends I made brought me into their community, shared food and drink, and told me all about what they were doing to address the issues they faced in Sweden, such as the rise in white nationalism, how to navigate the heavily taxed beer (solution: make it yourself!), and, of course, climate change. Their radical hospitality showed me that I had found a home away from home. Speaking and organizing with *Juliana v. United States*, I have traveled to such places as Norway, Germany, and Switzerland, and I never fail to find a community of anarchists and punk houses that make the most unfamiliar places feel like home. From the metal bars in the United Kingdom to the Hambach Forest Occupation in Germany, I have always found a welcome place, because the community I dedicated myself to back home is based on a philosophical and geographical foundation that is so much bigger than the Pacific Northwest. Fighting for a world free of racism, sexism, and exploitation (as we play angry soundtracks of revolution) is a fight that recognizes no borders.

While anarchism and Christianity may have differences, there are similarities, as well. Since I was a child growing up in the church, I've had experience serving the homeless, marching for gender rights, and protesting the misuse of the Earth. Now I've found a different community, but I'm still fighting against the same things. While UCC churches across the country have been dedicating Sundays to talking about climate change and showing their support for our case, my punk friends are organizing bike race benefits for Our Children's Trust.

Often when talking to others about organizing, I hear the same kinds of questions: What gives you hope? Don't you sometimes feel like giving up? My answer is this: I will not give up even in the face of the most hopeless future. History makes a few things clear: there have always been issues, no one person has ever fixed them, and for every social problem that's getting better, something else is getting worse. While we celebrate the abolition of slavery, it also paved the way for the prison industrial complex. The #MeToo movement is helping society hold powerful men accountable for gender violence, but our president bragged about committing sexual assault during his candidacy and still won. We have developed affordable solar panels, but the government used military vehicles against Standing Rock to clear the way for yet another pipeline expansion. Because we have so much to work on, social justice will always be a way for me to find meaning in life.

Climate change may not be solved in my lifetime, and definitely not by me, but that's not the point. We have a choice: to let our narcissism envelop us and ignore issues we think we can't fix, or to join movements with passion rather than expectations. Finding purpose in my life is essential to understanding my future. Giving up doesn't help me; passion for my community does. From Moses in the Bible to Malcolm X in America, the links in the chain of social justice go back farther than we can ever see. We might not be around to witness the end of the exploitation of the Earth, but that doesn't mean we should stop fighting. Christians may call that faith, and perhaps it is. Faith, hope—whatever you call it—impels me to organize, which for me is about recognizing that the fight is infinitely bigger than myself, while at the same time staying grounded and present with the people around me in each fleeting moment. They are the links that remind me of the chain going hundreds of years into the past and, I hope, hundreds of years into the future.

Chapter Twenty-Two

Interview with Dr. Tink Tinker (wazhazhe/Osage Nation), PhD

By Leah D. Schade

Tink, you are a respected Osage elder among the urban Indian community of Denver, Colorado. Can you talk about how you have been called to your work of activism on behalf of American Indians?

For twenty-six years I ran an Indian organization called Four Winds American Indian Council on a pro bono basis while I was functioning as an academic professor. Over that time, I was working very closely with several *ieska* (what you would call "medicine people") on different reservations. Eventually a couple of *wanagi,* two eagles and a coyote, got my attention through no intention of my own and asked me to be *ieska* (interpreter) for them.

You see, our elders don't go to school for four years and get a master's degree in "Indian Divinity" and then set up shop as ministers. Their status is established through a lifetime of experience and then the people's experience of them. This special relationship with *wanagi* comes usually when they don't expect it and don't even necessarily want it. Many elders are hesitant to receive this relationship because it comes with such great responsibility. This relationship began for me during a ceremony when the coyote and eagles came to me. From that moment on, my responsibility was unrelenting because these *wanagi* were communicating with me so intensely.

You've written about the bitter irony of whites turning to American Indians to ask for wisdom to help rescue white people from the environmental jeopardy that they themselves caused. This has included centuries of slaughtering and oppressing First Nation peoples. Now that the climate crisis has become even more acute, can you share your sources of hope?

I am not a person who embodies hope. I am much more in league with my colleague Miguel De La Torre who fashions himself as a theologian of *no hope.* After 500 years of violence, invasion, genocide—all of which is ongoing—hope is not a viable category for me. Christians have a history of trying to make us like white people through the ongoing indoctrination of the "protestant[1] work ethic," capitalism, and assimilation to eurocentric culture. Indians would have to further compromise our cultural values to assent to a theology of hope. And besides, what Indians are experiencing today is a continuing, nonstop violation of what is left of our lands by euro-christian corporations—for instance, building pipelines against the wishes of local Native communities across their lands and mining sacred sites.

What I hear you saying is that when the dominant group strips the oppressed group of its hope, it cannot turn around and look to that group to rescue them when they are facing an existential crisis of their own making.

Yes. My colleague Vincent Harding, long before he died, really wanted me to join him in a venture called "The Council of Elders." It involved a wide variety of activists from across the continent, modeled after the international council of elders started by Desmond Tutu, Nelson Mandela, Jimmy Carter, and others. Many of them are old friends and allies of mine. But this council had as its goal the establishment of "true" democracy, whatever that is. In other words, this was to be a group of radical *hope* to reform or correct the system in the United States. I sadly had to tell Vincent that I simply could not buy into the goals and objectives of the group—even though I genuinely like the people involved. I would necessarily be leaving my people behind.

Can you share examples of ways in which hope has been stripped from your people?

Whites tell stories that Indians welcomed them onto their land. In fact, we were coerced and forced into giving up our land in order to save our people. We had no choice but to move our people to the reservations. Even then, the christians never kept their word. Thousands upon thousands were massacred throughout the land. As the leader Red Cloud once said, "The white people have made my people many, many promises. They only kept one. They promised that they would take our land."

The Osage Nation signed something like seven treaties in forty-nine years for the promise of health, education, and welfare, all of which have been violated by the U.S. government. Now this same government is in the process of trying to erase all Indians by saying we've got to stop the welfare state. But it's in the treaty! It's *rent payment*! It's not welfare.

Never forget that your wealth, the home that you live in (whether you own it or rent it), the salary you earn, comes from the theft of Indian land, the extraction of resources from that Indian land, and the oppression of forced labor on African peoples who were kidnapped and brought here to work this land. And then, in order to keep labor prices low, Asian peoples were brought in to com-pete with African people after the Civil War. All of this so that your christian people might have and keep all the more. When you're on the receiving end of that land and wealth, you might see it as "God's great gift." But in reality, it is a tragedy. When you're on the receiving end of that oppression from the christians, their God is an abject oppressor and not at all a savior.

Do you see any chance for elected leaders to right the wrongs that have been perpetrated against your people?

Just the opposite. For instance, what would any politician do about the Treaty of Ruby Valley and the intentions of Newmont Mining Corporation with regard to gold mining on Western Shoshone lands? The cyanide they use to begin the refining on site has poisoned the land and people. Then there is the uranium mining on Native lands in New Mexico and Arizona. And the Rio Tinto Zinc Corporation's copper mine in central Arizona that will hollow out a whole sacred Apache mountain before caving it in as refuse. Even the telescope they built on top of Mt. Graham required scraping the top of the mountain flat—over the objections of the San Carlos Apache. All the sacred energy of that mountain has now gone into retreat and is lost to the people. Indeed, Barbara Mann calls the last five centuries of Christian colonialism "a 500-year organized crime spree." Unfortunately, it's still going on. No potential american government has or will have the energy or the spirit to oppose this military-industrial phalanx. We Natives are projected to continue to lose our lands and our lives—unless we move to the cities and become like white people, leaving our cultures and love of the land behind us.

Does that mean you have given up?

No. I continue to resist, though more sedately since turning seventy. But still without hope.

So my asking you for a word of hope is yet another example of whites wanting to appropriate the Native American perspective to extract some kind of wisdom for our white christian project. Your words are meant to call us to accountability and justice. But another of my colleagues has pointed out that we don't get to appropriate your despair, either.

That's also true. What I've told Indian people all along is that we've got to remember the tragedy of colonialism. And part of what's happened to us is that our own minds have been colonized. Our task now is to decolonize our own minds. To break loose from the shackles with which the missionary has burdened us. Even our languages have been practically erased. We need to get rid of the colonizer's language and recover the deep meaning of our own languages. So many Indian reservations have language recovery and language preservation programs. We need to teach this to our children.

In this late period of colonialism, we are struggling to reconstruct our identity over and against all the colonialist and missionary pressures that have tried to coerce us into becoming like them. We are told, "You would be okay if you could just be like we are, do things the way we do them, see things the way we see them." But that's the problem. We *don't* see the world the way the Dakota Access Pipeline people see it, or any of the extractive industries that have exploded during this late christendom era.

Because of the plethora of other religions and the rise of atheism and the "nones" (those who claim no religious affiliation), some say we are actually in a post-christendom era. What impact do you think that has on interfaith dialogue about these issues?

This culture is still euro-christian to its core. Even if you are atheist, you are defining yourself over and against the predominant christian ethos and mythology. That makes you, at best, a christian atheist. The reigning euro-christian mythology of, for instance, the military-industrial complex begins with the first three chapters of Genesis in which humans are given *dominion*—that's where we get the *dom* of christen*dom*. It has come to mean *domination.* This is how U.S. foreign policy sees the world. But it's not how American Indians see the world. We are kin with all the animals, with the trees, with the mountains, with all living beings. There is no superbeing or superdeity that rules over all, and humans do not have ascendancy of import over the rest of life. We are not anthropocentric.

Christian missionaries told us that our word *wakonda* means "god." They reinterpreted the word *wakon* to mean "holy" or "sacred." They tried to re-define our own language. But *wakon* really means "the ability to give life or take life." So *wakon* has a universal quality about it. All of us are *wakon* in that sense, and every place is *wakon*—not just the church. And *wakonda*, far from meaning some hierarchical superpower, is the word to describe that cosmic energy that touches us all, every living being from rocks to people. Strangely enough, this has more in common with modern astrophysics than with any christian notion of a higher power.

So, this recapturing of our own languages means that we Natives relate to everything differently than christians. Once when I took my young daughter out for a walk, she was fascinated with bunnies and those roly-poly bugs. I told her, "They are your cousins. You have two-legged family. But these are your family, too." It's all *relationship.*

How does this principle of relationship shape your interactions with the natural world?

For example, Native folk need to make ceremony before they can cut down a tree. At sun dance, the people go out to that tree as a group, make offerings and talk to the tree before they take its life. They ask it to carry the people's thoughts and concerns into the spirit world.

How far does this concept of relationship extend? For instance, does it apply to the food you eat?

Even the things on your plate that you eat are your relatives. Incidentally, this is why we don't believe in nonviolence. Because we know we are going to take part in an act of violence every time we eat lunch. Something will have to die in order for us to live. So we have to have a way of doing ceremony before we can take the life of those things we're going to consume. Even the vegetables are our relatives. Corn is our mother. And you're violating "the sacred" (to use that colonial word) every time you eat corn just as much as when we eat steak. So we have to do ceremony for those corn mothers. Corn, beans, and squash, the Three Sisters, are the mothers of all people. We must give them respect. They give their life for us in order to sustain us.

This is such a different way of viewing the world than most americans are used to. We consume things so mindlessly. We don't give a second thought to the chicken in our nuggets or the trees that became our cabinets.

That's a major difference between christians and American Indians. We don't have the kind of worldview that would enable us to clear-cut a forest like Boise-Cascade does in the Pacific Northwest. No, we're out there nurturing the forest. We're paying homage to it and building relationship with it. So if I need wood for a fireplace, I need to do the appropriate ceremony to collect the wood, knowing that I've done my part to restore life, harmony, and balance.

But the story we're often told about American Indians is that the tribes were violent and engaged in war.

Yes, we had military engagements. And do you know how long they lasted? Sometimes a whole day! There might be disputes on the borders between the different nations. But then it was settled quickly, and the two sides parted. A battle was not meant to extract fealty or to decimate the enemy. That was the euro-christian way—for instance, the Thirty Years War between catholics and protestants to determine whose understanding of the death of Jesus was to rule Europe. Even so, we had to have ceremony before we went out to fight. Those ceremonies would last for thirteen days, and we knew someone could get hurt or even killed. Today there is no ceremony. The white leaders do not go into a retreat before deciding whether or not to go to war. They are wars for extraction, especially for oil.

That's another example of something we consume mindlessly—energy. The oil and gas from the shale. The coal from the mine. Perhaps if we had had ceremony for using these energy sources, our consumption might be slower, more thoughtful.

Each year, my daughter's teachers in elementary school try to tell her that the rocks are inert, that they do not move. She has to correct them: rocks *are* living beings. Of course they move! They just move more slowly because they are more settled in their relationships. Two-leggeds need to learn from the rocks instead of trying to extract from them. Learn to be settled. We need to feel more deeply our relationships to our ancestors, this world, and each other.

This settled-ness is sorely missing from our culture. We're so frenzied, so focused on growth and acquiring the newest and the most.

European culture is deeply rooted in the emergence of the radical individual, a notion especially canonized during the Renaissance when artists began to sign their works. For Indians, it's about *us*, not about *me* and *mine*. What has happened on this continent, and indeed, in the rest of the world, is that christian colonialism has stretched across the globe and continues to be an unending tragedy with no relief in catharsis.

As a christian preacher and homiletics professor, I'm rethinking how we convey the message about climate change based on what you've been saying here.

What bothers me persistently is that christian preaching and liturgies invariably tend to be romantic, the opposite of tragic or recognizing the tragedy of modern life. Maybe christians would do well to explore the tragic instead of trying to make people feel good. An awful lot has been done wrong in the name of christianity. And we have a long way to go before we begin to make right what was made so terribly, terribly wrong in these last five hundred years.

Your words are convicting and so necessary for me and others to hear. As our planet is facing the kind of fate that First Nation peoples all over the world have suffered over the last five centuries, how do you go forward?

Read Indian novels. My favorite is Leslie Silko's book *Ceremony*.[2] Indian novels tend to be relatively depressing because they capture the experience of colonization pretty acutely. And yet, somehow they all end with a kind of unbelievable, unexplainable, undefinable, unjustifiable optimism. Because we embrace life. All of life. Thirty years ago, when people were talking about the potential for environmental disaster on this planet, the Elders told me that we are coming upon the day when the Earth is finally going to get rid of this species called "two-leggeds." But, they told me, the Earth, our Grandmother, will continue and will heal after we are gone.

I would imagine you get a lot of pushback when you say that. It sounds misanthropic.

My white colleagues tell me, "We don't want human beings to be destroyed." I correct them: "Not: be destroyed. Rather: destroy themselves." You're making that choice in what you eat, in what you drive, the clothes you wear. It's that extractive principle in white christianity that is leading to this devastation. It's not just the extraction of oils and uranium. But the extraction of labor, the extraction of resources and wealth.

Six of the ten poorest counties in the United States are American Indian Reservations. We suffer a horrendous state of poverty. We have a 60 percent unemployment rate that is five times that of African Americans and ten times that of white americans. It is the Third World in the middle of the First World.

So what word do you give to those who are dealing with what white Christendom has done? What word do you have for them? Not for us, but for those who have had everything taken from them. How do you go one more step?

I tell them that it really is going to be okay. Indians are clear on this. We affirm *life* in the midst of poverty, in the midst of death. At Pine Ridge. At Crow Creek. At Rosebud. The Earth will do just fine. Our Grandmother will survive.

I am humbled by your words, Tink. Thank you.

Thank you for your attention to these matters and for hearing what I have to say.

NOTES

1. Editors' note: In keeping with Dr. Tinker's request, the use of the lower case for such adjectives as "english," "christian," "european," and so on, is intentional. Tinker explains: "While nouns naming religious groups might be capitalized out of respect for each Christian—as for each Muslim or Buddhist—using the lower case "christian" or "european" for adjectives allows readers to avoid unnecessary normativizing or universalizing of the principal institutional religious quotient of the christian euro-west. Likewise, I avoid capitalizing such national or regional adjectives as american, amer-european, european, euro-western, and so on. I also refer to north America. It is important to my argumentation that people recognize the historical artificiality of modern regional and nation-state social constructions."

2. Leslie Marmon Silko, *Ceremony* (New York: Penguin Books, 1977).

Chapter Twenty-Three

Working Up Hope

Tim DeChristopher

The story of Easter Island is so well known that it has become a cultural trope about collapsing societies. By the seventeenth century, the people of Easter Island had exhausted their natural resources. They overfished their waters and hunted their birds to extinction. They enslaved their people to make stone idols of their gods. As their natural resources dwindled, they used the last of their trees to transport ever greater idols into position to be worshipped. As the threats and signs of their unsustainability mounted, they doubled down on the practices and perspectives that had caused their problems. Ultimately, the people of Easter Island died out while idolizing their gods. The collapse of Easter Island society serves as a warning that human nature may prevent us from responding to the climate crisis in a rational and productive way. Maybe when things get bad enough, our society will make a dramatic shift and we will do what needs to be done to protect our shared survival. But maybe not.

In contrast are the people of Karphi, whom I first heard about in a sermon by Unitarian Universalist minister Rev. Liz Lerner Maclay. Around the seventeenth century BCE, Karphi was a peak sanctuary city on the island of Crete. After Minoan culture was ravaged by natural disasters and war, Karphi became the last Minoan holdout. On a desolate mountain peak, Karphi was subject to harsh environmental conditions that made survival difficult. Still, even after the Minoan capital was conquered, the people of Karphi held on for another two hundred years and scrupulously maintained the worship of the Minoan gods.

The important part of their story is what the people of Karphi did when they realized that life in their community had become environmentally unsustainable: they buried their gods and walked away. There is no evidence that war, disaster, or disease finally finished off the people of Karphi. Rather, the

147

gods whom they had so carefully worshipped were placed in stone coffins, and the people walked off into the lineage of Mediterranean cultures.

As Rev. Maclay acknowledged, that act of burying their gods might seem like the ultimate moment of despair. She invoked T. S. Eliot:

> This is the way the world ends
> This is the way the world ends
> This is the way the world ends
> Not with a bang but a whimper.

But Rev. Maclay also recognized that the act of walking away reflects a sense of possibility and active hope. The people didn't cling to a dying society. Instead they were willing to let go of everything they knew and to move on in an act of ultimate courage. Beyond the comfort of their idols and their national identity, they had faith in the possibility of creating new lives for themselves in an entirely unknown world.

From their isolated vantage point in Karphi, they could not have had much actual reason for hope. They *made* their hope by walking. When they carried out the radical act of burying their gods, they did so without hope. When they let go of the only home they had ever known, they did so without hope. But even in the absence of hope, they had the courage and the will to take the first step and start walking.

As we enter the wild, uncharted territory of climate catastrophe, I find an important lesson in the example of Karphi. Much of my work revolves around the paradox of needing to act to fight climate change while knowing that we have already lost the fight. I am often asked to name what gives me hope, or what I can say to give others hope, when we have already reached a stage of the climate crisis that likely makes catastrophic impacts inevitable. As a Unitarian Universalist, there is little eschatology on which I can rely that will make everything okay in the end. Our religious calling centers on building the kingdom of God here on this Earth. Sometimes in response to the question of hope I make something up, perhaps about our ability to build a more humane world out of the ashes of this one, or maybe something about our resilience in caring for each other on our death beds. But these answers usually feel inadequate because the questions themselves seem so absurd to me. How could anything "give" me hope? And how could I "give" it to others? Like faith, hope is inseparable from our own actions. It isn't given; it is grown. Waiting to act on climate change until we have hope is like waiting to pick up a shovel until we build up calluses on our hands. The hope never arrives until we get to work.

But that first step is a doozy. The climate movement often tries to ease people into this struggle with comfortable consumer changes, one-click activism, and a vision of green economic growth. Imagine instead trying to woo new recruits with a message of, "Bury your gods and stride forth into the unknown!" Perhaps there is a reason that the story of Karphi is not often invoked as an example. Even the model of Easter Island is more comforting because it only demands from us a lazy cynicism that nothing will ever change. Cynicism unto death is far easier than burying our gods and moving on to a new way of living.

But of course, the people of Karphi did not actually bury any god. They buried only stone idols of ideas they worshiped. The spirit of life went with the people on their journey. The sparks of divinity within themselves continued to burn, and the dynamic love that flowed within and among them continued to flow. They were still sewn up in the fabric of destiny through which their lives and actions caused ripples to impact the entire interconnected web of existence. From this vantage point thousands of years later, we can recognize that God was still with them. But it's clear that incredible courage was nonetheless required in order to bury the idols through which they had understood their purpose and relationship to that which gave higher meaning to their lives. For centuries up to that point, the worship of those idols had structured the meaning of their lives and had likely carried them through countless previous bouts with despair. Burying those idols was an act of faith that their entire history and culture were not the limits of their destiny.

At this point of climate crisis when our civilization is no longer sustainable, what are the gods that we are called to bury in order to move forward? What are the idols through which we understand our purpose and our relationships—particularly those idols that have brought us to this brink of climate and ecological catastrophe? Here in the United States, we are and always have been a capitalist and imperialist nation built on domination. These are the practices and perspectives that have caused the climate crisis, and I believe they are the gods that must be buried in order for us to move on.

The god of capitalism, and its attendant demigods of rampant individualism, consumerism, and perpetual growth, is the central structure of American civic religion. Because capitalism is rooted in the ever-increasing extraction, production, and sale of goods, this is a worship that we can no longer afford. As many good economists have pointed out, infinite growth is not possible on a finite planet. In order to maintain the capitalist illusion of endless growth for as long as possible, citizens have been turned into consumers, with our primary identity and system of meaning defined by our habits of consumption. Because alienated people make better consumers, a pervasive ethic of hyper-individualism has been cultivated and foisted onto us by those who are committed to perpetuating capitalism. These mentalities of individualism and consumerism are now so deeply rooted in our culture that even when we want to affect major change and fight climate disruption, we first think of our role as individual consumers. While liberating ourselves from harmful consumption can be a valuable part of self-purification, if we are not liberating ourselves *to* our other roles as citizens, community members, and children of God, we remain stuck in the isolated and disempowered identity of consumer.

We can also no longer afford to worship the god of American Empire. In service of a false belief that we could take from other places to provide for ourselves, the United States has treated the world like our own resource colony for more than a century. But now climate change has revealed the truth that we cannot ravage other places without hurting ourselves as well. Our wars for oil weren't just stealing from the countries we invaded; they were also stealing from our own future. Some of us actually may be driven away from the physical places we live, like the people of Karphi. Others of us may be lucky enough to avoid migrating in the face of catastrophic climate impacts but will still feel the effects of these impacts on our lives. In any case, all of us will be forced to abandon the mental notion of the American Empire in which we live. As the greatest collective problem in history, climate change reveals the lie at the heart of American exceptionalism. It turns out that we are, in fact, living on the same interconnected planet as everyone else, and that we can't address this crisis without global cooperation. In a future shaped by climate refugees, it is perverse to continue worshipping the notion of arbitrary borders that determine which of God's children have a right to live and which do not. And yet, this notion of nationalism is so ingrained in our culture that even some of those who are trying to fight climate change are peddling a narrative that America needs to "beat" China in the race for clean energy.

The many-faced god of domination is woven throughout our culture and is the only type of power that is recognized by mainstream society. Since European people first came to this continent, domination defined the way we related to the indigenous population and the native landscape. While this mentality has always meant disaster for marginalized people, the climate crisis makes clear that our domination of nature was a dangerous lie for everyone. At this point, when we have almost certainly committed to catastrophic levels of climate disruption, the one thing we can be sure of about the future is its unpredictability. Such a future demands humility and a level of resilience that can only come from diversity. Like any ecosystem or complex system of any kind, homogeneity is a liability we can only afford in times of tranquility and predictability. Resilience to disruption is rooted in strong connections and openness among a wide array of people with diverse ideas. Since mutual vulnerability is now unavoidable, we have to learn to harness the power of community and lead with mutuality. This is the steady power of cooperation rather than the fleeting victory of competition. It is the wisdom of being open to the voices of others rather than the certainty of having the right answers. It is a power rooted not in our own strength, but in our empathy with others. And yet, domination is so idolized in our culture that some people respond to the climate crisis by proposing a technocratic vision, one-size-fits-all solutions, and centralized decision-making.

When we begin to bury these idols, we begin to liberate ourselves to walk the path on which we develop hope. For me, this path has led to a decade of civil disobedience against the fossil fuel industry, including two years as a political prisoner for my resistance. Every step on that path has helped grow the hope on the palms of my hands and the soles of my feet. When I de-emphasize my identity as a consumer and begin to live into my roles as citizen and community member, I feel hope forming like the calluses on my hands. When we actively resist the xenophobia and racism at the root of American exceptionalism, we develop the perspective to see new possibilities that only became visible once we step out of our fortress sanctuary. When I let go of the insecure need to dominate and instead accept, even embrace, my vulnerability, I begin to see that new ways of being are possible.

I can't claim to have buried all these idols in my own life, but I can testify to the fact that all of my real hope has been built up from the small ways in which I have begun to stop worshipping these false gods. I cannot say what future lies in front of us if we do abandon these gods. But it is clear that continuing to worship these gods of greed and domination does not serve us. They are worse than stone idols, and there is no hope in anything they can offer. We have to have faith that regardless of what our chaotic and radically disrupted future holds, the spirit of love that flows through us and among us will continue to make our lives rich with meaning. As scary as it is, we have to bury our idols and move on.

Chapter Twenty-Four

Questions to Ponder
and a Spiritual Practice

QUESTIONS TO PONDER

1. Kiran Oommen openly and courageously expresses many doubts: whether or not God exists, whether or not we will survive the age of climate disruption, whether or not there is hope. Yet, he says, "I have an intrinsic need to *find* purpose, and that is essentially tied up in community." Where and with whom have you found your purpose and "passionate, organizing community"? Do you gravitate more toward young people in Kiran's generation, middle-aged folks, or seniors? Is it important to you to build community across generations? What support have you been able to draw from your friends in this work? How have you supported others?
2. "Never forget that your wealth, the home that you live in (whether you own it or rent it), the salary you earn, comes from the theft of Indian land, the extraction of resources from that Indian land, and the oppression of forced labor on African peoples who were kidnapped and brought here to work this land." Tink Tinker's words call us to account in the midst of our climate activism. Do some research about the history of indigenous peoples and African Americans in the place where you live. What disturbs you? What humbles you? What surprises you? How might you reconsider your relationship with the natural world in light of Tinker's words about honoring our relationships with all our relatives, human and other-than-human?
3. Tim DeChristopher contrasts the fates of two ancient societies—Easter Island and the people of Karphi. About the latter, he says, "Beyond the comfort of their idols and their national identity, they had faith in the possibility of creating new lives for themselves in an entirely unknown world." What are the idols of our society that have led to this climate crisis? How have they tempted or seduced you? What are the false gods that

you need to let go of? In what ways has your country's national identity been a hindrance or a help in mobilizing to address climate change? If, as DeChristopher says, hope "isn't given; it is grown," what might you do that would not only help to heal the Earth but also help your hope to grow?

A SPIRITUAL PRACTICE

Praying with Strong Feelings

No one has written more cogently than Joanna Macy about what she calls the need to "honor our pain for the world."[1] Exercises like her "Breathing Through"[2] can become staples of our spiritual life as we learn to experience our feelings without letting ourselves drown in them or be swept away. Opening our hearts to strong emotions like grief and moral outrage breaks through the "psychic numbing"[3] that Robert J. Lifton noticed in his study of the survivors of the bombing of Hiroshima. Theologian and biblical scholar Walter Brueggemann likewise speaks eloquently about the prophetic power of grief to critique and confront injustice and to open a path to new life. Brueggemann shows how the prophet Jeremiah, for one, articulates not only his own pain and the pain of his community, but also the pain of God.[4] Jeremiah invites the people to enter and experience God's grief, and also to hope in God's promises.[5]

Are we willing to share our honest feelings with God? Because no single image can encompass the divine Mystery, all our images of God are necessarily provisional and incomplete. Still, some images of God are more helpful than others. If we are burdened by images of God that evoke only fear of rejection, punishment, or abandonment, then we will never feel sufficiently safe to disclose our real self (including our feelings) in prayer. On the other hand, if we explore imagining God as a friend, our relationship with God is more likely to grow in truthfulness, trust, vulnerability, and intimacy. We are more likely to encounter the God of love.

The practices and reflection questions below can be explored at different times, alone or with others.

- What feelings are easy for you to express to God? What feelings do you tend to stifle or avoid?
- Where do you feel the pain of the Earth? Where do you hear the groaning of God's Creation? What are the losses you need to mourn? What are the tears you need to shed?
- Write or draw a prayer of lament, protest, confession, or intercession.
- Is there an image of God that allows you to feel safe? Can you imagine God as a friend? A friend is someone with whom you can be yourself.

Perhaps you can imagine God gazing on you with kindness. Perhaps you can imagine God sitting beside you, eager to listen. If you are not drawn to a personal image of the Divine, you might imagine God as perhaps the air around you, the ground beneath you, or a fire within you. Alternatively, you might imagine the Divine as a loving Presence beyond any imagery at all. In the company of that Presence, you are free to feel whatever you feel, without fear of being judged or shamed. In expressing your grief about ecocide and injustice, you may be sharing in God's own grief.

• Are you willing to let your anger, fear, guilt, and grief become a place of encounter with God? As you sit in prayer, allowing feelings to arise and pass through, notice the love that is embracing you, whatever you feel. . . . Breathe it in. Breathe it out. . . . Let your heart be open. . . . Don't hold on to anything. Let the feelings move through you. . . . Stay close to the One who holds you—and the whole Creation—in love.

NOTES

1. Joanna Macy and Chris Johnstone, *Active Hope: How to Face the Mess We're in without Going Crazy* (Novato, CA: New World Library, 2012), 76.

2. Macy and Johnstone, *Active Hope*, 73–74.

3. Robert Jay Lifton, *The Broken Connection: On Death and the Continuity of Life* (New York: Basic Books, 1979), 112.

4. Walter Brueggemann, *The Prophetic Imagination* (Philadelphia: Fortress Press, 1978), 44–61.

5. Brueggemann, *Prophetic Imagination,* 68.

Section VII

GRIEF, LOVE, AND TREES

Section VII Introduction

This final section roots and rises in experiences with trees and other living entities. While all three authors share moving reflections on what it means to sit with the profound grief that accompanies our growing eco-awareness, they each discover something else as well. Christina Leaño finds both solace and spiritual renewal in the wisdom of a giant sequoia tree. Roger S. Gottlieb cultivates perspectives that transcend despair and reframe our reasons for engaging in the work of protecting and preserving the fragile, precious lives that remain on this planet. And Margaret Bullitt-Jonas emerges from the cycle of addiction with a message of lament, liberation, and love.

Chapter Twenty-Five

Contemplating Creation

Wisdom from a Sequoia

Christina Leaño

The entire material universe speaks of God's love, his boundless affection for us. Soil, water, mountains: everything is, as it were, a caress of God.

—Pope Francis, *Laudato Si': On Care for Our Common Home*[1]

I knew immediately which tree I wanted to spend twenty minutes with in conversation. I was in the middle of the Arnold Arboretum in Boston on a "forest bathing" retreat. Our group of ten people had spent the summer morning immersed in practices to unplug from our usual device-driven lives and experience the healing power of nature. Now we were invited to spend twenty minutes alone with a new tree friend and see what might emerge from the relationship.

Earlier we had walked slowly through a meadow noticing its smells and sounds. We had felt the cold water of a trickling stream between our fingers, and experienced nature as if with new eyes. The premise of forest bathing—called *Shinrin-Yoku* in Japan—is to be open to the forest "medicine" for the soul, not merely for our own benefit, but for the healing of all life. As the Association of Forest and Nature Guides states, forest bathing "is a deeply relational practice, characterized by a sense of loving and tender connection. This connection leads naturally to an ethic of tenderness and reciprocity."[2]

Nature immersion practices such as forest bathing are not new. Intimate relationships with the more-than-human world have been part of human experience for millennia and are still evident today in indigenous cultures around the world. Yet many of us have lost touch with this side of ourselves. Through intentional practices that open the senses and heart, forest bathing reminds us of who we are: members of a wider web of life.

As a Christian, the practices of forest bathing invite me into the same kind of intimate relationship with Creation that saints throughout the ages have cultivated. St. Francis is perhaps the most well known for doing this, being famous for talking to the birds and making peace with a murderous wolf. In his Canticle of Creatures, St. Francis calls the elements "Sir Brother Sun," "Sister Moon and the Stars," "Brother Wind," and "Sister Water," considering all of them members of his family.

In his recent encyclical *Laudato Si': On Care for Our Common Home,* Pope Francis invites us to experience a similar intimacy with the natural world. He quotes Scripture to show the biblical roots of this understanding of Creation: "Through the greatness and the beauty of creatures one comes to know by analogy their maker" (Wisdom of Solomon 13:5); indeed, "his eternal power and divinity have been made known through his works since the creation of the world."[3]

In *Laudato Si'*, Pope Francis explains that all animals, plants, elements, and people are to be seen as brothers and sisters, connected through the bonds of love and mutual responsibility. He goes even further to say that failing to appreciate the inherent beauty and value of each creature and person can lead to a danger of perceiving all of Creation—including other people—as existing solely for our own selfish purposes.

In the Arnold Arboretum, I walked slowly toward this towering beauty of a tree whose bark had a reddish shimmer. We were to approach our chosen tree as if it were a new friend: say hello, introduce ourselves, and wait for the tree to respond. We could then engage in a conversation or just sit in each other's presence with open senses and silence.

As I circumambulated the tree, I found the silver identification tag placed on most of the trees in the arboretum: *Sequoiadendron giganteum.* My heart lifted when I realized that I had chosen (or had been chosen by) a giant sequoia redwood. I felt a deep affinity to the redwoods as spiritual teachers. From 2008 to 2011, I lived in a Catholic Cistercian monastery in the middle of an old-growth redwood forest in Northern California. Driven by love of God and the contemplative life, I became a novice in this cloistered community while exploring a call to become a Catholic nun. During that time the redwoods became my companions, the holder of my secrets, and a source of strength from their centuries-old bark.

I leaned against the trunk of the sequoia. As I had with many of the redwoods in the monastery, I experienced this sequoia, too, as my mother, holding me with maternal strength. I felt her hard trunk supporting me, as I found a seat at her roots. I sat and listened.

In *Laudato Si'*, Pope Francis invites us "to hear both the cry of the earth and the cry of the poor."[4] As I opened to the presence of the sequoia, I began to hear the cries of Creation. A cave in my chest opened as I felt a depth of sorrow about the climate crisis. I saw images of island and coastal communities being swallowed up by the tides. Swaths of rain forests being razed to create palm oil plantations and ranches for the cattle industry. Millions of people starving because of droughts and desertification. I felt the pain of my own participation in economic and energy systems that contribute to the destruction of our planet.

Tears fell down my cheeks as my despair grew. I felt this tree emanate a sadness of the realities facing our planet, of what we humans have done through our blindness and unbridled selfishness. I turned around to touch her soft wisps of red bark. My new friend felt so steady, seemingly able to hold all of the pain and sorrow within her strong trunk. I looked up into the branches that stretched from her trunk and saw glimpses of blue sky. In desperation I beseeched her, "What am I to do? How am I to respond to the immensity of this crisis?"

And then an unexpected image of a turkey appeared in my mind's eye. It was a memory from when I lived in the monastery—a turkey roosting in the middle of a redwood tree. One dusk while I was walking through the monastery grounds, I caught sight of a small flock of turkeys gathered at the edge of a field. One turkey took off running, as if on a dare, with its balloon-like body heaving up and down on its grayish legs. Then in what appeared to defy the laws of physics, the turkey's body started to rise from the ground, first a few inches and then a few feet, while the turkey flapped its huge wings. Slowly angling upward toward the edge of the forest, the turkey ascended until its feet grasped one of the lower branches of the redwoods.

It did not stop there. The turkey slowly began to hop up the tree, branch by branch. Each ascent was accompanied by a flutter of wings, and then a pause before the turkey flapped to the next level. After a few minutes, seemingly satisfied with its position, the giant bird nestled some fifty feet above the ground, beyond the reach of bobcats, raccoons, foxes, or other predators. The seven other turkeys followed suit, and by nightfall I was able to see their silhouettes sitting high in the tree branches, safe. Until that moment, I hadn't even known that turkeys could fly! Seeing a turkey roost in a tree was like seeing the impossible become possible.

With this memory of a turkey roosting came a message from the sequoia tree: "Branch by branch." My new friend seemed to be telling me that my task, like that of the turkey, was to slowly ascend one branch at a time. I need not solve the whole crisis, but just move branch by branch, step by step.

As I continued to gaze up into her branches, I felt the relief of the invitation. The overwhelming reality of the climate crisis had not disappeared, but

I felt that I better understood what my response needed to be. I was not called to solve everything, but simply to do my part, one branch at a time.

I bring to mind those words—"branch by branch"—and the image of a turkey hopping branch by branch, whenever I start to feel overwhelmed. Those words serve as a refuge, a reminder to trust and to do my part—and to continue to listen to Creation for guidance on what next steps I need to take to protect the living world entrusted to our care.

In *Laudato Si'*, Pope Francis states, "Rather than a problem to be solved, the world is a joyful mystery to be contemplated with gladness and praise."[5] What would it look like if we took these words to heart? It would not absolve our responsibility to do everything within our power to help our global economies transition from being fossil fuel–based and rooted in consumerist models. It might, however, change our stance to one of deeper listening to the love and guidance that our planet is offering us if we stop, listen, and receive.

As part of my work with the Global Catholic Climate Movement, I now invite people to enter into a process that is similar to my forest bathing retreat. In what we call *Laudato Si'* retreats, we remind participants that "God has written a precious book, whose letters are the multitude of created things present in the universe,"[6] and we are called to meditate on these words of love through contemplating Creation.

Through a process of "linger, listen, and love," participants are invited to walk in nature at an easy pace and to linger whenever they feel that a particular flower or tree might be calling to them. Then they are invited to engage in dialogue with their new friend and to discover what questions and answers naturally arise. When it is time to part, participants are invited to offer love—perhaps through prayer, gesture, or touch—as a way of giving thanks for the time spent together, the wisdom received.

Retreatants have reported profound insights arising from time spent communing with Creation. One person was reminded of the years of environmental work she had done with a friend, helping her to appreciate the history of her work and the role that others had played in it. Another person received a message to trust where she was right now, in the midst of a life of committed action.

I have also found that connecting to Creation need not even take place in nature. In a spiritual direction session, a health-justice activist was dealing with the challenging question of how to know how much action was enough, given the seemingly endless needs of the world. Through a guided meditation, an image of a spring-fed creek in her childhood home came to her mind. The metaphor of running water being fed by a hidden source gave her comfort and clarity.

I continue to be nurtured and strengthened through my relationship with Creation. It can happen when I receive a loving glance from a neighborhood tree outside my apartment. Or when I get inspired by the beauty of a sunset during a drive home. When I get overwhelmed with the climate crisis, I often will go outside and ask the sky, a flower, or a tree what to do. Sometimes, I am reminded of the turkey hopping in the tree and to just take things one branch at a time. But mostly, Creation tells me to "keep going, we need this" and "you can do this." Creation watches, cries, and encourages us, inviting us to listen to her to and to trust.

Strengthened in this way by Creation, I continue on the path, heeding this message: branch by branch. And with Creation I chant inwardly one of my other favorite phrases from *Laudato Si':* "For we know that things can change."[7] Thanks to the power of the Holy Spirit and the guidance of God speaking to us through Creation, I live in this faith that things *can* change— the impossible can become possible.

NOTES

1. Pope Francis, *Laudato Si'—Praise Be to You: On Care for Our Common Home* (Vatican: Libreria Editrice Vaticana, 2015), paragraph 84, http://w2.vatican.va/content/francesco/en/encyclicals/documents/papa-francesco_20150524_enciclica-laudato-si.html.

2. "The Practice of Forest Therapy," The Association of Nature and Forest Therapy Guides and Programs, https://www.natureandforesttherapy.org/about/practice.

3. Pope Francis, Laudato *Si'*, paragraph 13, referencing Romans 1:20.

4. Pope Francis, *Laudato Si'*, paragraph 49.

5. Pope Francis, *Laudato Si'*, paragraph 12.

6. Pope Francis, *Laudato Si'*, paragraph 85.

7. Pope Francis, *Laudato Si'*, paragraph 13.

Chapter Twenty-Six

Living with Environmental Despair

Roger S. Gottlieb

Several years ago, at a small, highly interdisciplinary conference on the environmental crisis, an internationally respected expert on the oceans confided to us all, in a bleak tone, "Everything I've studied to get my big deal reputation, everything: it's all dead or dying." He hadn't stopped working, he told us, because he didn't know what else to do with his life. But he had no hope that anything, or at least very much, could be done about the destructive mix of climate change, industrial pollution, encroachment by development, and noise pollution (which affects sea mammals).

This man was afflicted by environmental despair, and with good reason.

"Despair" is often defined as the loss or absence of hope, but I think it is a deeper and more complex state of mind that can arise in all of us who take the environmental crisis seriously. Psychologist Miriam Greenspan defines *despair* as a disruption of the relationship between what we thought the world was and what we find it to be and a corresponding loss of meaning that stems from the fact that our beliefs and actions no longer seem to connect, to make sense, with what the world actually is.[1]

Here are a few lines of thought I have turned to for help in dealing with my own environmental despair. Sometimes they give me comfort. At others, they seem like whistling in the dark. Despair, I suspect, will for the indefinite future be a permanent part of an awakened consciousness. But perhaps it need not be the whole story.

KNOWLEDGE

It is perhaps a measure of how bad the environmental crisis can make us feel that we might turn for solace to the simple fact of human ignorance.

167

As much as we think we know what the future will hold, we really don't. It might, indeed, be much worse than we imagine. Rather than climate change and ecosystem breakdown killing millions of people, they might kill a billion or more. Modern civilization, rather than just being made more difficult in countless ways, might completely collapse. Ecosystems, rather than losing keystone species and diminishing in biodiversity, might simply be erased: deserts replacing forests, wetlands, and meadows; the oceans reduced to jellyfish and algae blooms.

At the same time, things might get considerably better. As long as human creativity and the ability to learn from the past persist, social changes might arise that we, from our current vantage point, simply cannot envision. In my own lifetime I have seen what I consider progressive, beneficial changes take place that I couldn't have even conceived of, let alone believed were possible.

One obvious example is the legalization of gay marriage. Another is the ascension of women to powerful, influential positions in academia, medicine, and government. A third is the recent manner in which revelations of sexual misconduct and abuse have ended the reign of abusive men in entertainment, politics, and media.

The general point is that no matter how bad things look—and they certainly do look bad—we cannot be sure what they will be like in the future. Emotionally, this means that while grief, fear, and anger are perfectly rational, at least the part of despair that stems from a sense of certainty about the future is not.

I am not suggesting that things will work out or that progress is inevitable. Such beliefs are easily refuted by even a casual awareness of humanity's cruelties and irrationalities. Rather, I am proposing that it is possible to live in the present without certainty about the future—either about how awful it's going to be or about how things will turn out alright. At least when applied to large social transformations, such certainty is virtually always a mistake. Despite how attractive either may be, neither hope nor hopelessness is epistemologically appropriate.

Of course, hopelessness and unjustified hope do share the advantage of attenuating deep anxiety about the future. If we are certain about what is coming, we need no longer be anxious. We can rest in the happy confidence that no matter how bleak things look today, everything will turn out well in the end; or we can rest in despair and refuse to be tortured by continually dashed hopes.

Given the limitations on what we can know about the future, such anxiety, I believe, is a permanent feature of our collective predicament. What is called for, then, is perhaps neither hope nor hopelessness—but courage to live with the fear.

Where could that courage be found?

IN THE HOSPITAL

Let us imagine (God forbid) that someone you dearly love—say, your mother—is terribly ill, confined to a hospital bed, perhaps hooked up to a breathing machine or simply extremely weakened. Confused and dispirited by pain and increasing disability, she faces a future that is completely in doubt. There is a good chance that she will die. Yet recovery is still possible. Certainty either way is impossible, both because of the nature of the illness and because of the many times that medical prognosis has proved dead wrong.

What would you do? Would you sink into a passive, unmoving despair because things look so bad—especially after one of the nurses confided to you that there really wasn't any hope for your mother and you'd better "make all the necessary arrangements"? Or would you rest in a kind of exaggerated certainty that "Of *course* Mom will get better; she just has to!"

Note that both of these emotional and cognitive postures direct your emotional energy to the future, to the outcome, to what things will be like when the anxiety over the future is over—because the future has arrived. But is the future where you would want to spend your mental time? Is that what you would want to dominate your consciousness?

Perhaps not. Especially if you really do love your mother and want to express that love not just in obsessions about the future, but about what is going on *now*. Not if connection to her in the present is more important—personally, morally—than whatever the future will bring. I think you would spend as much time in the hospital as you could: making her as comfortable as possible, conferring with doctors, perhaps reading and singing to her, or just holding her hand. You would want do what you could, for as long as you could, to express your love, and to be in her presence while she was still alive.

What this has to do with environmental despair is simply this: the illnesses and damage with which humans are afflicting nature, and themselves, have no certain future. But to the extent that we feel connected to trees and birds and our relatives and neighbors and perhaps just life in general, wouldn't we want to embody that connection in active love and care, *whatever* the future holds? As we would want to comfort our own mother even if she will be dead in three days, so wouldn't we want—knowing that the future is in doubt and nothing is forever—to try to make a carcinogenic pesticide illegal, clean up a polluted stream, liberate some dogs from labs, or keep snowmobiles out of a wilderness area?

In other words, perhaps we don't need to know what the future holds in order to express our love—in activism—*now*.[2]

What is that love made of? In part, if you have a reasonably good relationship with your mother, it's made of a deep sense of appreciation for who she is and the part she has played in your life. The precise contours of her face, the unique sound of her voice, her laugh, even the sound she makes walking across a room. Whatever the future may hold, these have been real, deeply important, and treasured—even if now her breathing is labored or she has cancerous tumors in her body.

And despite the many dimensions of the environmental crisis, comparable things are true of our natural environment. It, too, can be appreciated for the part it has played in our life. It, too, has been essential to our being alive at all. The term "Mother Nature" might be a cheap cliché, but it also contains a simple truth. What else, after all, gave birth to us?

Thus the future—along with our hope or hopelessness about it—can recede just because of what you *can* be certain about: the many forms of value of the beings who are suffering right now; how you feel about them; and what you want to do to ease their pain and, just maybe, make a brighter future for a few of them.

And this is all the more urgent because Mother Nature is not suffering from "natural" causes—but from countless instances of human-caused assault: overuse, needless pollution, monstrous quantities of wasted resources. We are, all of us (but to widely varying degrees), part of an environmental regime that is systematically an attack on all of life—nonhuman and human alike.

IT'S ENOUGH THAT IT EVER WAS

A complete and unshakable despair over the present and the future is only possible if we forget our gratitude for the present. Reality can be reduced to nothing more than unmitigated horror only if the delights and gifts that we have *already* experienced are treated as commonplace, ordinary, not very important, and—above all—taken for granted. In this mental state, we seem to think, "Of course I have had a, b, c, and d, and still have e, f, and g . . . but what's *really* important, what's actually crucial, what in fact will occupy every last bit of my mental and emotional energy, is that h, j, and k have died. And in the future x, y, and, worst of all, z, will happen."

Now I am certainly not denying that x, y, and z are terrible environmental realities that may very well unfold. Or that countless such realities have occurred already. Avoidance and denial are psychological states that are emotionally exhausting and a betrayal of any serious moral identity. They are also deeply implicated in the ethical calamities of our time. The severity of the environmental crisis, and our own part in contributing to it, make informing ourselves a moral obligation.

What I am suggesting is that our mental and emotional energy is finite. We can only think about so much at a time.

Why spend it all on imagining the terrible future, especially since that future, while likely, is not certain? Why not reserve some energy for the miracle of life that has already existed, and that despite everything continues to exist in the present? Why not celebrate that we ourselves have been alive, and that so have redwood trees, dolphins, and butterflies—as well as the fungi and bacteria who liberate necessary nutrients from dead bodies.

Is the existence of the universe itself something that we can "rationally" regard as just something to be expected, a matter of course, as in: "Of course there is a universe; now let's pay attention to all the ways in which it isn't what I want it to be"? While it might be a widespread psychological tendency to continually notice what's lacking, is that a sensible or ultimately satisfying way to respond to life?

There are growing numbers of psychological theorists who have been exploring what is commonplace among the world's spiritual traditions: gratitude. It's no secret that gratitude is an essential component of happiness. I believe that gratitude can also be an important psychological—or, if you will, spiritual—element in enabling us to carry on with a modicum of contentment and even joy despite what we are doing to nature, including our fellow humans.

Gratitude is often a choice. Among the possible objects of consciousness there are a host of things to feel miserable about—and with good reason. But there are, I am suggesting, a least some things to feel good about as well. And often it will be a matter of conscious decision, a pattern supported (or not) by regular spiritual or psychological practices that inspire and sustain gratitude. We can decide that gratitude is possible, that it makes sense, and that we want it to be part of our lives. And then we will need to use techniques—ranging from prayer and meditation, to writing and music, or petting our dogs, or looking carefully at ducks on a pond or leaves on a tree—to make it a reality.

I call the personal commitment to such practices a spiritual choice, though other words (psychological, moral, personal) might be used as well. By "spiritual" I mean a fundamental commitment to a form of life that downplays the conventional ego's focus on its goals and desires, and instead cultivates such virtues as compassion, love, and, yes, gratitude.

Choosing such a spiritual (or moral, or psychological) response to the environmental crisis depends on our believing that we, like all other beings, deserve a modicum of happiness and contentment—*even* if the world is going to hell and human beings are experiencing widespread misery from environmental as well as many other causes.

We might think: By what right do we celebrate some tree in our backyard or a nearby park while rain forests are being cut down to make grazing land for beef cattle, and the pine trees of the American West are being devoured by beetles that are thriving due to climate change?

The answer is: no right at all, for contentment is not a matter of right and wrong, but of a fundamental disposition toward reality. The truth is that we do not save one tree or sparrow by being unhappy. Our despair does not remove a single toxic chemical from the air or improve the life of one animal trapped in a lab. If we take nature as our inspiration, note that a tree will not waste its energy on anxiety over the future or bitterness for its fate, even as the chain saws approach. It will simply give all of its being to life until its life expires or is taken from it.

Can we do the same?

Along with our reasonable and deeply felt fear and grief, can we appreciate, just as deeply, that the universe has existed and that we got to be alive?

As we grieve all the losses that have already taken place, and all the ones yet to come, can we say, "It's enough that it ever was—and that we got to be part of it"?

If we can, then despair will be real and potent, but will not dominate.

It's enough that it ever was.

Enough for what? For life to have arisen. And for us to continue, for as long as we can, to both celebrate and protect it.

NOTES

1. Miriam Greenspan, *Healing through the Dark Emotions: The Wisdom of Grief, Fear, and Despair* (Boston: Shambhala, 2003).

2. That we ourselves are in all probability contributing to nature's illness, and what our moral responsibility is in that regard, is an issue I am systematically avoiding here. For a detailed answer, see Roger S. Gottlieb, *Morality and the Environmental Crisis* (New York: Cambridge University Press, 2019).

Chapter Twenty-Seven

Love Every Leaf

Rev. Dr. Margaret Bullitt-Jonas

If you'd seen me then, you might have said I was alive. In 1982 I was thirty years old, a graduate student at a premier university. I breathed. I walked, talked, accomplished things, made decisions, and got the job done. But I wasn't truly alive—only partly. I was only marginally present in my own life. Caught for years in the grip of an eating disorder, in secret I ate compulsively, fasted and exercised compulsively, and lived inside a world of self-doubt and shame. As every addict knows, addiction involves ignoring and overriding the body's needs. It didn't matter what I felt—I defied the messages of my body. So what if I was tired, lonely, angry, or sad? Whatever I felt, I swallowed it down with food and went out for another long run. Pummel and punish the body—that was my motto.

I wasn't literally killing myself. I wasn't putting a gun to my head or jumping off a bridge. But every time I closed the curtains, hid out with a dozen donuts, and gulped them down in one sitting, I was committing psychic suicide. There aren't many people as filled with despair and self-hatred as an addict who can't stop doing what she's doing, even though she knows she's sliding down a path that leads to death. I didn't want to be on that path, but despite my best efforts—diets, calorie counting, and fervent vows—nothing worked for long. I kept on anesthetizing myself, going mindless and numb.

Through the grace of God, I hit bottom. A combination of circumstances interrupted my headlong rush to oblivion. Just when the pain of refusing life was becoming intolerable, a colleague died abruptly. Her apparent suicide forced me to ask myself: was that how my own life would end? On April 13, 1982, I stumbled into a Twelve-Step meeting and asked for help. I needed a Higher Power that could save me from myself and set me on a better path. The choice was clear: make peace with my body or die.

I tell that story in my memoir, *Holy Hunger*—how I chose life and learned the difficult art of listening to my body and living within its limits.[1] I learned to rest when I was tired, to eat only when I was hungry, to weep when I was sad, to speak up when I was angry, and to allow feelings to pass through me as freely as weather that passes across an open sky. The tools, steps, and practices of the Twelve-Step program helped me to make peace with the closest bit of Nature entrusted to me: my own body.

Here is the story my memoir didn't tell: recovering from an eating disorder set me on fire with a question. Who was this Higher Power that had just saved my life? Looking for an answer, I completed my doctorate at Harvard in Russian and comparative literature and headed straight to seminary. I met and eventually married a man who was on his own spiritual journey. Buoyed by his love and support, I was ordained in the Episcopal Church in June 1988, which happened to be the month that climate scientist James Hansen testified to the Senate that global warming was a threat to life on Earth. A new question began to take form, one that has animated me ever since: If God can help an addict like me to make peace with her body, is it not possible that God can help humanity to make peace with the body of Earth?

For surely as a species we are on a fast track to death, laying waste to the living world around us as if there were no tomorrow. The juggernaut of our economic system is devouring Mother Earth, relentlessly seeking to extract and burn every drop of oil, every ounce of coal, and every trace of so-called "natural" gas. Pummel and punish the body—that's the system's motto. Like an addict, this system is insatiable. It knows no limits. It rejects any regulation and restraint as it strains forward to grab the next buck.

An addictive system can't think clearly. It hides behind excuses and denial, distraction and delay. It prefers to talk about the problem rather than to take meaningful action. It insists that no other way of life is possible. *It's too late to change. We can't stop—not yet, anyway. Not now. First let's drill more oil wells, build more pipelines, extract more tar sands, blow off more mountaintops, and cut down more trees. Let's find out how much more petroleum we can burn, how much more carbon pollution we can pour into the atmosphere, and how much more money we can make before we blow past the tipping point that propels the world into climate chaos.*

For years we thought we could get away with it, but now we know where that path leads: to unraveling the web of life and to the possible collapse of civilization. We might as well be sawing off the branch on which we sit of the tree of life. We may look like we're alive, but in fact we are only marginally present. Caught in the feverish grip of addiction, we're ignoring and overruling Earth's needs. More than one Secretary General of the United Nations has deemed our present course "suicidal."

Will we finally choose the path of life? Will we come to our senses in time to stabilize our disrupted climate? Will humanity decide to relinquish what Alcoholics Anonymous calls "self-will run riot" and to accept the limits that restore life? I take these questions personally, because I believe that the same mysterious Presence who saved my life and who daily restores my life is now calling me to urge my fellow humans to do the same. Call it an intervention. Call it a plea from one addict to another: liberation is possible! Together we can set a course to a more just and sustainable future. Together we can turn from death to life.

In 1989, after the Exxon-Valdez oil spill, I delivered the first sermon I'd ever preached (or heard) about protecting God's Creation. Since then I've been writing, speaking, and preaching about the climate crisis with increasing urgency and focus. I've been organizing and participating in Christian and interfaith worship services, prayer vigils, conferences, marches, and rallies; traveling to Standing Rock and to the White House; lobbying; risking arrest; and leading retreats on spiritual resilience and resistance for diocesan clergy, seminarians, and the wider public. These decades of effort spring from one source: my relationship with the liberating God of love who saved my life almost forty years ago.

Just as much as I want to keep the living world alive, I want to keep my soul alive. Protecting the outer landscape requires that I protect my inner landscape, too. I find ongoing energy and courage to rise up and safeguard life only if I am spiritually grounded. The intention to stay inwardly alive—awake, aware, sensitive to self and others, and responsive to the leadings of Spirit—must be renewed every day. That's where prayer and meditation come in. To whom do I pray? To the divine Father/Mother who creates life and who loves every inch of Creation, the God who made an "everlasting covenant" with every living creature on Earth (Genesis 9:16). To Jesus Christ, whose mission statement was clear: "I have come that they may have life, and have it abundantly" (John 10:10). To the Holy Spirit who longs, even more than I do, to "renew the face of the earth" (Psalm 104:31).

In times like these, our prayer may need to be expressive and embodied, visceral and vocal. How else can we pray with our immense anger and grief? How else can we pray about ecocide, about the death that humanity is unleashing upon Mother Earth and upon ourselves? How else can we break through our inertia and despair, so that we don't shut down and go numb? Like the addict finally coming to terms with her physical, emotional, and spiritual needs, it is important to protect our human capacity to feel our emotional responses to the crisis, for that is how we stay inwardly vital and alive. Just as important, our emotions can become a source of energy for constructive action to address the emergency. Prayerful lament and protest can be an act of resistance, a way of shaking off the dominant consumer culture, which prefers that we stay too busy, dazed, and distracted to feel a thing.

My prayer takes many forms. Recently a company began cutting down trees in the woods behind my home, clearing space for co-housing, an intentional neighborhood of private homes that share a common area and develop a strong sense of community. I'm all for co-housing and I've met some nice people who plan to live there, but, honestly, I grieve the trees. They have been companions to me and sources of beauty. They are living presences that I know play a vital role in keeping life on Earth intact. Scientists tell us that we can't stabilize the climate unless we save trees. Preserving forests is critical to combating climate change.[2]

Because of all this, I've taken to praying outdoors. I go outside, feel the good earth beneath my feet and the wind on my face, and I sing to the trees—to oak and beech, hemlock and pines. Making up the words and music as I go along, I sing my grief to the trees that are going down, and my grief for so much more—for what we have lost and are losing, and for what we are likely to lose. I sing my outrage about these beautiful old trees being cut to the roots, their bodies chipped to bits and hauled away to sell. I sing my fury about the predicament we're in as a species. I sing my protest of the political and corporate powers-that-be that drive forward relentlessly with business as usual, razing forests, drilling for more oil and fracked gas, digging for more coal, expanding pipeline construction, and opening up public lands and waters to endless exploitation, as if Earth were their private business and they were conducting a liquidation sale. I sing out my shame to the trees, my repentance and apology for the part I have played in Earth's destruction and for the part my ancestors played when they stole land and chopped down the original forests of the Native peoples who lived here. I sing my praise for the beauty of trees and my resolve not to let a day go by that I don't celebrate the precious living world of which we are so blessedly a part. I'm not finished until I sing my determination to renew action for trees and for all of God's Creation.

I feel God's presence when I pray like that. I dare to believe that the Spirit who longs to renew the face of the Earth is praying through me. Praying like this leaves me feeling more alive, connected with myself and with the world I love.

So our prayer may be noisy and expressive, or it may be very quiet. It may be the kind of prayer that depends on listening in stillness and silence with complete attention: listening to the crickets as they pulse at night, listening to the rain as it falls, listening to our breath as we breathe God in and breathe God out, listening to the inner voice of love that is always sounding in our heart. A discipline of contemplative prayer or meditation can set us free from the frantic churn of thoughts and feelings and enable our spirit to rest and roam in a vaster, wilder space.

We can pray alone and we can pray together, for we need communal rituals that address our fear of death and give us courage to trust in a life greater than death. We need rituals that ask us to name our guilt and regrets, that grant us forgiveness, and that give us strength to set a new course. We need rituals that remind us of our essential connection with each other, with the rest of the created world, and with the unseen Source of all that is. We need rituals that remind us of how loved we are, how precious the world is, and what a privilege it is to be born in a time when our choices and actions make such a difference.

Once upon a time we thought we could divide people into two camps: "spiritual" people who pray, meditate, and contemplate the world's beauty; and "activist" people who organize and advocate to address the world's suffering. One group cared only about personal transformation; the other, only about societal transformation. It's high time to heal that false split, for we need people who long for fullness of life, both for themselves and for all beings. We need people who cultivate deep inner wisdom and also take bold, creative action on behalf of life on this planet.

Back when I studied Russian literature, I came to cherish a passage from Dostoevsky's novel *The Brothers Karamazov*. "Love every leaf," says Father Zossima, the Russian Orthodox abbot. He is describing from his deathbed the perception of reality that inspired his life, and the ethics that flow from that perception.

> Love all God's creation, the whole and every grain of sand in it. Love every leaf, every ray of God's light. Love the animals, love the plants, love everything. If you love everything, you will perceive the divine mystery in things. Once you perceive it, you will begin to comprehend it better every day. And you will come at last to love the whole world with an all-embracing love.[3]

We live in a pivotal moment of the planet's long history, a moment, in the words of theologian Elizabeth Johnson, when "the future of the tree of life is now at the mercy of human decision and indecision."[4] Like an addict who has lost control, we will be restored to sanity only by a power greater than ourselves. Addiction is a disease of isolation that can be healed only by reclaiming membership in a larger community. Sometimes only love can stop a person, group, or society from self-destruction—the kind of tough love that holds the addict accountable and refuses to settle for a catastrophic status quo. Sometimes only love can set us free to take action when death surrounds us and we have no promise or even likelihood of success.

Standing among logs and stumps that just hours ago were a living forest, I pick up a beech tree leaf. I cradle it in my palm, marveling at its veins and stem, color and shape. A message resounds in this leaf: *Here is the world in its beauty*. A second message comes: *Here is the world in its fragility*. I cup my hand gently around the leaf as I hear its final message, an urgent appeal: *Here is the world in its need and longing to be healed.* I hear in the leaf the same supplication that sings in my own deep core: *Choose life!*

If I could, I would place this leaf in your hands. I would ask you to join me in singing our love to this leaf. "And [we] will come at last to love the whole world with an all-embracing love."

NOTES

1. Margaret Bullitt-Jonas, *Holy Hunger: A Woman's Journey from Food Addiction to Spiritual Fulfillment* (New York: Knopf, 1998; Vintage Books, 2000).

2. John J. Berger, "We Can't Save the Climate Without Also Saving the Trees. Scientists Agree: Preserving Forests Is Critical to Combating Climate Change," *Sierra Magazine*, October 29, 2018, https://www.sierraclub.org/sierra/we-can-t-save -climate-without-also-saving-trees.

3. Fyodor Dostoevsky, *The Brothers Karamazov,* trans. Constance Garnett, rev. and ed. Ralph E. Matlaw (New York: W. W. Norton, 1976), 298.

4. Elizabeth A. Johnson, *Ask the Beasts: Darwin and the God of Love* (London: Bloomsbury, 2014), 285.

Chapter Twenty-Eight

Questions to Ponder
and a Spiritual Practice

QUESTIONS TO PONDER

1. All three authors in this section recount powerful personal stories that compel them to work for climate justice. What is the story of your relationship with the natural world—that is, your eco-biography? For example, how did you relate to nature when you were a child? How has that relationship changed as you've grown? Where are the sacred places in Creation that call to you—and call for you to be their advocate?

2. The chapters at the end of this collection describe poignant experiences with grief and how nature (including trees) generously offers comfort, wisdom, and healing. Christina Leaño, for example, talks about "forest bathing" and communing with trees and other Earth-kin in a practice of "linger, listen, and love." In what ways have your experiences with nature healed you? How could you make yourself more available to healing from the natural world?

3. This section begins with a quote from Pope Francis saying, "The entire material universe speaks of God's love, his boundless affection for us," and it ends with a call from Dostoevsky to "love every leaf." How has the natural world spoken to you of God's love? What helps you become aware of how loved you are and how loved all beings are? How important to your spiritual life is cultivating love for God's Creation? How might a more lively, even passionate, relationship with the natural world affect your commitment to working toward solutions for the climate crisis and healing Earth?

A SPIRITUAL PRACTICE

Meeting Nature as Thou

What kind of relationship do we presently have, and wish to have, with the natural world? Spirituality is fundamentally about our capacity for relationship. In what spirit are we turning toward the other, encountering the other, communicating or communing with the other? In his classic book *I and Thou*, Jewish philosopher Martin Buber contrasts two kinds of relationship, using the example of a tree: I-It (in which we treat the other as a thing, an object to use) and I-Thou (in which we experience the other as a subjectivity). When we encounter a Thou, we are vulnerable and willing to be changed. Buber emphasizes the vitality of authentic encounter. As he puts it, "All real living is meeting."[1]

Do we see God's Creation only in terms of its use to us (tree = lumber; meadow = acres to sell for development) or are we open to the possibility that God wants to speak to us through tree, sun, and wind, through grass, rock, and sparrow?

- Go outdoors for a contemplative walk in a natural setting. Or if you are in an urban area, notice the ways that nature finds a foothold in a crack in the sidewalk, for example, or in a nest within the nook of a building. Walk slowly and in silence, letting each step draw you into the present moment. Notice smells, sounds, textures, and colors. Feel the wind. Bless the ground with each step. Breathe.
- Where does your body want to encounter the body of Earth? Allow a particular place to draw your attention. Get to know your sacred place. Notice everything you can. Gaze, touch, smell, and listen.
- Let a natural element or living being draw your attention. First, try being in an I-It relationship with it. Notice what happens to your awareness. Then try being in an I-Thou relationship with it. You might ask: *Who are you? What is it like to be you? Who am I to you? Who are you to me? What can I learn from you? What can I give you? How is God present here?* Take your time. Notice what happens.
- Let your mind grow quiet. Allow God to address you in the stillness.
- Before you leave, is there a gift you wish to offer—perhaps a prayer or a blessing?

NOTE

1. Martin Buber, *I and Thou*, trans. Ronald Gregor Smith (New York: Charles Scribner's Sons, 1958), 11.

Bibliography

Abdul-Matin, Ibrahim, and Keith Ellison. *Green Deen: What Islam Teaches about Protecting the Planet.* Leicestershire, UK: Kube Publishing, 2010.

Adams, Carol J. *Ecofeminism and the Sacred.* New York: Continuum, 1993.

Antal, Jim. *Climate Church, Climate World: How People of Faith Must Work for Change.* Lanham, MD: Rowman & Littlefield, 2018.

Bass, Diana Butler. *Grounded: Finding God in the World, A Spiritual Revolution.* New York: HarperOne, 2015.

Bauman, Whitney A., Richard R. Bohannon II, and Kevin J. O'Brien, eds. *Grounding Religion: A Field Guide to the Study of Religion and Ecology.* New York: Routledge, 2011.

Benstein, Jeremy. *The Way into Judaism and the Environment.* Woodstock, VT: Jewish Lights, 2006.

Bernstein, Ellen, ed. *Ecology and the Jewish Spirit: Where Nature and the Sacred Meet.* Woodstock, VT: Jewish Lights, 2000.

Bernstein, Ellen. *The Splendor of Creation: A Biblical Ecology.* Cleveland, OH: The Pilgrim Press, 2005.

Berry, Thomas. *The Christian Future and the Fate of Earth.* Edited by Mary Evelyn Tucker and John Grim. Maryknoll, NY: Orbis Books, 2009.

Berry, Thomas. *The Sacred Universe: Earth, Spirituality, and Religion in the Twenty-First Century.* Edited by Mary Evelyn Tucker. New York: Columbia University Press, 2009.

Bingham, Sally G., ed. *Love God, Heal Earth.* Pittsburgh: St. Lynn's Press, 2009.

Boff, Leonardo. *Cry of the Earth, Cry of the Poor.* Maryknoll, NY: Orbis Books, 1997.

Bouma-Prediger, Steven. *For the Beauty of the Earth: A Christian Vision for Creation Care.* Grand Rapids, MI: Baker Academic, 2003.

Bullitt-Jonas, Margaret. *Christ's Passion, Our Passions: Reflections on the Seven Last Words from the Cross.* Cambridge, MA: Cowley Publications, 2002.

Bullitt-Jonas, Margaret. *Holy Hunger: A Woman's Journey from Food Addiction to Spiritual Fulfillment*. New York: Knopf, 1998; Vintage Books, 2000.

Bullitt-Jonas, Margaret. *Joy of Heaven, to Earth Come Down: Meditations for Advent and Christmas*. Cincinnati, OH: Forward Movement, 2012, 2013.

Carroll, John E., Paul Brockelman, and Mary Westfall, eds. *The Greening of Faith: God, the Environment, and the Good Life*. Hanover, NH: University Press of New England, 1997.

Chase, Steven. *Nature as Spiritual Practice*. Grand Rapids, MI: William B. Eerdmans, 2011.

Christie, Douglas E. *The Blue Sapphire of the Mind: Notes for a Contemplative Ecology*. New York: Oxford University Press, 2013.

Chryssavgis, John, ed. *Cosmic Grace, Humble Prayer: The Ecological Vision of the Green Patriarch Bartholomew I*. Grand Rapids, MI: William B. Eerdmans, 2003.

Cohen-Kiener, Andrea, ed. *Claiming Earth as Common Ground: The Ecological Crisis through the Lens of Faith*. Woodstock, VT: SkyLight Paths, 2009.

Dahill, Lisa E., and James B. Martin-Schramm, eds. *Eco-Reformation: Grace and Hope for a Planet in Peril*. Eugene, OR: Cascade Books, 2016.

Dear, John. *They Will Inherit the Earth: Peace & Nonviolence in a Time of Climate Change*. Maryknoll, NY: Orbis Books, 2018.

Delio, Ilia, Keith Douglass Warner, and Pamela Wood. *Care for Creation: A Franciscan Spirituality of the Earth*. Cincinnati, OH: Franciscan Media, 2008.

Foltz, Richard, ed. *Worldviews, Religion, and the Environment: A Global Anthology*. Belmont, CA: Wadsworth/Thomson, 2003.

Francis [Pope]. *Laudato Si'—Praise Be to You: On Care for Our Common Home*. Vatican: Libreria Editrice Vaticana, 2015.

Gottlieb, Roger S. *Engaging Voices: Tales of Morality and Meaning in an Age of Global Warming*. Waco, TX: Baylor University Press, 2012.

Gottlieb, Roger S. *A Greener Faith: Religious Environmentalism and Our Planet's Future*. New York: Oxford University Press, 2006.

Gottlieb, Roger S. *Morality and the Environmental Crisis*. Cambridge: Cambridge University Press, 2019.

Gottlieb, Roger S. *The Oxford Handbook of Religion and Ecology*. New York: Oxford University Press, 2006.

Gottlieb, Roger S., ed. *This Sacred Earth: Religion, Nature, Environment*. 2nd ed. London: Routledge, 2004.

Greenspan, Miriam. *Healing through the Dark Emotions: The Wisdom of Grief, Fear, and Despair*. Boston: Shambhala, 2003.

Grim, John, and Mary Evelyn Tucker. *Ecology and Religion*. Chicago: Island Press, 2014.

Hamma, Robert M. *Earth's Echo: Sacred Encounters with Nature*. Notre Dame, IN: Sorin Books, 2002.

Harris, Melanie L. *Ecowomanism: African American Women and Earth-Honoring Faiths*. Maryknoll, NY: Orbis, 2017.

Harvey, Andrew, and Carolyn Baker. *Savage Grace: Living Resiliently in the Dark Night of the Globe*. Bloomington, IN: iUniverse, 2017.

Hayhoe, Katharine, and Andrew Farley. *A Climate for Change.* New York: Faith Words, 2009.

Hessel, Dieter T., and Rosemary Radford Ruether, eds. *Christianity and Ecology: Seeking the Well-Being of Earth and Humans.* Cambridge, MA: Harvard University Press, Harvard University Center for the Study of World Religions, 2000.

Jenkins, Willis. *Ecologies of Grace: Environmental Ethics and Christian Theology.* New York: Oxford University Press, 2008.

Johnson, Elizabeth A. *Women, Earth, and Creator Spirit.* New York: Paulist Press, 1993.

Kearns, Laurel, and Catherine Keller, eds. *Ecospirit: Religions and Philosophies for the Earth.* New York: Fordham University Press, 2007.

Khalid, Fazlun. *Signs on the Earth: Islam, Modernity and the Climate Crisis.* Leicestershire, UK: Kube Publishing, 2019.

Levy, Natan, David Shreeve, and Harfiyah Haleem. *Sharing Eden: Green Teachings from Jews, Christians and Muslims.* Leicestershire, UK: Kube Publishing, 2013.

Macy, Joanna, and Chris Johnstone. *Active Hope: How to Face the Mess We're in without Going Crazy.* Novato, CA: New World Library, 2012.

Macy, Joanna R., and Molly Young Brown. *Coming Back to Life: Practices to Reconnect Our Lives, Our World.* Gabriola Island, BC, Canada: New Society Publishers, 1998.

McFague, Sallie. *A New Climate for Theology: God, the World, and Global Warming.* Minneapolis, MN: Fortress Press, 2008.

McKibben, Bill. *Eaarth: Making a Life on a Tough New Planet.* New York: Henry Holt, 2010.

McKibben, Bill. *Falter: Has the Human Game Begun to Play Itself Out?* New York: Henry Holt, 2019.

Moe-Lobeda, Cynthia D. *Resisting Structural Evil: Love as Ecological-Economic Vocation.* Minneapolis, MN: Augsburg Fortress, 2013.

Moore, Kathleen Dean. *Great Tide Rising: Towards Clarity and Moral Courage in a Time of Planetary Change.* Berkeley: Counterpoint, 2016.

Moore, Kathleen Dean, and Michael P. Nelson, eds. *Moral Ground: Ethical Action for a Planet in Peril.* San Antonio, TX: Trinity University Press, 2010.

Moseley, Lyndsay, and the staff of Sierra Club Books, ed. *Holy Ground: A Gathering of Voices on Caring for Creation.* San Francisco: Sierra Club Books, 2008.

Nagy, Luqman. *Green Muslims: The True Custodians of the Earth.* Riyadh: Maktaba Daru-us-Salam, 2010.

Nash, James. *Loving Nature: Ecological Integrity and Christian Responsibility.* Nashville: Abingdon Press, 1991.

Nasr, Seyyed Hossein. *Religion and the Order of Nature.* New York: Oxford University Press, 1996.

Northcott, Michael S. *A Moral Climate: The Ethics of Global Warming.* Maryknoll, NY: Orbis Books, 2007.

Rasmussen, Larry L. *Earth-Honoring Faith: Religious Ethics in a New Key.* New York: Oxford University Press, 2013.

Rhoads, David M., ed. *Earth and Word: Classic Sermons on Saving the Planet.* New York: Continuum, 2007.

Robb, Carol S. *Wind, Sun, Soil, Spirit: Biblical Ethics and Climate Change*. Minneapolis, MN: Fortress Press, 2010.

Roberts, Elizabeth, and Elias Amidon, eds. *Earth Prayers from Around the World: 365 Prayers, Poems, and Invocations for Honoring the Earth*. New York: HarperOne, 1991.

Rowthorn, Anne, ed. *Feast of the Universe: An Interfaith Sourcebook of Ecological Spirituality from the World's Great Cultures and Religions*. Leeds, MA: LeaderResources, 2009.

Rowthorn, Anne, and Jeffrey Rowthorn, eds. *God's Good Earth: Praise and Prayer for Creation*. Collegeville, MN: Liturgical Press, 2018.

Ruether, Rosemary Radford. *Integrating Ecofeminism, Globalization, and World Religions*. Lanham, MD: Rowman & Littlefield, 2005.

Santmire. H. Paul. *Nature Reborn: The Ecological and Cosmic Promise of Christian Theology*. Minneapolis, MN: Fortress Press, 2000.

Schade, Leah D. *Creation-Crisis Preaching: Ecology, Theology, and the Pulpit*. St. Louis, MO: Chalice Press, 2005.

Schade, Leah D. *Preaching in the Purple Zone: Ministry in the Red-Blue Divide*. Lanham, MD: Rowman & Littefield, 2019.

Silko, Leslie Marmon. *Ceremony*. New York: Penguin Books, 1977.

Stephenson, Wen. *What We Are Fighting for Now Is Each Other: Dispatches from the Front Lines of Climate Justice*. Boston: Beacon Press, 2015.

Swedish, Margaret. *Living Beyond the "End of the World": A Spirituality of Hope*. Maryknoll, NY: Orbis Books, 2008.

Taylor, Bron, and Jeffrey Kaplan, eds. *The Encyclopedia of Religion and Nature*. 2 vols. New York: Continuum, 2008.

Taylor, Sarah McFarland. *Green Sisters: A Spiritual Ecology*. Cambridge, MA: Harvard University Press, 2007.

Tucker, Mary Evelyn, and John Grim, series eds. *Religions of the World and Ecology*. 10 vols. Cambridge, MA: Harvard University Press, 1997–2004.

Vaughan-Lee, Llewellyn, ed. *Spiritual Ecology: The Cry of the Earth*. Point Reyes, CA: Golden Sufi Center, 2013.

Wallace, Mark I. *Green Christianity: Five Ways to a Sustainable Future*. Minneapolis, MN: Fortress, 2010.

Wallace-Wells, David. *The Uninhabitable Earth: Life After Warming*. New York: Tim Duggan Books, 2019.

Waskow, Arthur, ed. *Torah of the Earth: Exploring 4,000 Years of Ecology in Jewish Thought*. Vol. 1: *Biblical Israel & Rabbinic Judaism*; Vol. 2: *Zionism and Eco-Judaism*. Woodstock, VT: Jewish Lights, 2000.

Wheatley, Margaret J. *Who Do We Choose to Be?: Facing Reality, Claiming Leadership, Restoring Sanity*. Oakland, CA: Berrett-Koehler Publishers, 2017.

White, Lynn Townsend, Jr. "The Historical Roots of Our Ecologic Crisis." *Science* 155, no. 3767 (March 10, 1967): 1203–7.

Yaffe, Martin, ed. *Judaism and Environmental Ethics: A Reader*. Lanham, MD: Lexington Books, 2001.

Scripture Index

Index

350-ppm carbon dioxide levels, xxvi
350.org, 123, 185

Abraham, xx, 46
Abrahamic faiths, xx, xxviii
activism:
    balancing demands of, 41, 99, 118;
    bonding and building community, 7,
    8, 40, 103; Civil Rights (*See* Civil
    Rights Movement); climate and/or
    environmental, 3, 7, 8, 29, 37, 39,
    55, 81, 133, 153; as devotional or
    religious practice, 7, 23, 39–40, 99,
    169; different forms of, 55; interfaith
    (*See* interfaith cooperation);
    LGBTQ (*See* LGBTQIA issues);
    Native American (*See* Native
    American issues); spiritual/religious
    roots of, xxviii, 8, 23, 39–40, 99,
    137, 139.
    See also civil disobedience; protests
addiction, 32, 34, 159, 173–74, 177
African American issues and climate
    change, 63–68, 69–74, 89–94,
    95–102, 153
air pollution. *See* pollution
Alabama, 66, 95
alternative energy. *See* energy,
    alternative forms of/renewable

American Indian. *See* Native American
    issues
anarchist punk movement, 135, 138
anger. *See* emotional responses to
    climate crisis
Antarctica, xxvi, 31, 96
animals, x–xi, xvii, xxvi, xxvii, 11, 19,
    20, 38, 77, 114, 142, 162, 171, 177.
    See also birds; extinction
anti-nuclear movement, 118, 124, 135
anxiety. *See* emotional responses to
    climate crisis
apocalypse, apocalyptic, 17, 84
Arctic ice melting, 17, 18
Arctic National Wildlife Refuge,
    drilling in, xxiv, xxv
asthma, relation to air quality, 64–66
Athanasius of Alexandria, 113, 115
atmosphere, climate change and, xvii,
    xxi, xxiii, 19, 32, 59, 91, 136, 174
Auschwitz. *See* World War II

balance:
    atmospheric gases, carbon dioxide,
    and, xxi, 57; finding personal
    balance, 41; as ordained by God, 13,
    91; with and within nature, 12, 70,
    91, 143
Baptist. *See* Christianity, Baptist

187

About the Contributors

Huda Alkaff is the founder and director of Wisconsin Green Muslims, a grassroots environmental justice group formed in 2005. An ecologist with higher education degrees in conservation ecology, sustainable development, and science/environmental education from the University of Georgia, she taught environmental studies courses at the University of Wisconsin Oshkosh. She spent two decades working as an advocate for environmental justice, initiating Muslim and interfaith programs focused on energy and water conservation. Alkaff co-chairs the U.S. Climate Action Network's Socially and Economically Just Adaptation and Mitigation action team, leads the Wisconsin Faith Communities for Equitable Solar Initiative, and is a founding member of the Interfaith Earth Network of Southeast Wisconsin and Wisconsin Interfaith Power & Light. She also serves on the national Greening Ramadan Team. Alkaff received the 2015 White House Champions of Change for Faith Climate Leaders recognition and the 2018 Wisconsin Association for Environmental Education Eco-Justice Award.

Jim Antal is a denominational leader, climate activist, author, and public theologian. He serves as Special Advisor on Climate Justice to the General Minister and President of the United Church of Christ. His book *Climate Church, Climate World* (2018) was featured on Earth Day 2018 in the Chicago *Tribune*. From 2006 to 2018, Antal led the 350 UCC churches in Massachusetts as conference minister and president. An environmental activist since the first Earth Day in 1970, he authored and was lead proponent of three national UCC resolutions: in 2013 the UCC became the first denomination to divest from fossil fuel companies; in 2017, in response to the U.S. pullout from the Paris Climate Accord, the UCC voted to resist all new fossil fuel infrastructure and to urge preaching on climate change; and in 2019, the UCC became the first Christian denomination to endorse the Green New Deal. He has also engaged the spiritual discipline of civil disobedience numerous times at the White House and elsewhere. Antal maintains a website: www. JimAntal.com.

Margaret Bullitt-Jonas is Missioner for Creation Care in the Episcopal Diocese of Western Massachusetts and the Massachusetts Conference, United Church of Christ. An Episcopal priest with a PhD in comparative literature from Harvard University, she taught courses on prayer, spirituality, addiction, and environmental justice at Episcopal Divinity School, served as chaplain for the Episcopal Church's House of Bishops, and spent twenty-five years in parish ministry. She has published numerous articles in books, journals, and anthologies, and is author of *Holy Hunger* (1998, 2000), *Christ's Passion, Our Passions* (2002), and *Joy of Heaven, to Earth Come Down* (2012, 2013). A long-time climate activist, she leads retreats in the United States and Canada on spiritual resilience and resistance in a time of climate crisis. She has been arrested in Washington, D.C., and elsewhere to protest expanded use of fossil fuels. In 2016 she received the Steward of God's Creation Award from the National Religious Coalition on Creation Care. Her website, www.RevivingCreation.org, includes blog posts, sermons, and articles.

John Chryssavgis is an author and theologian serving as archdeacon of the Ecumenical Patriarchate and theological advisor to the Ecumenical Patriarch. He is a clergyman of the Greek Orthodox Archdiocese of America. Born in Australia, he graduated from Athens University and Oxford University. His publications focus on medieval theology as well as on the history of the Eastern Church. His interests embrace the areas of spirituality and ecology. Chryssavgis co-founded St. Andrew's Theological College in Sydney, where he also taught at the University of Sydney. In 1995, he was appointed Professor of Theology at Holy Cross School of Theology and directed the Religious Studies Program at Hellenic College. He has also taught at the University of Balamand in Lebanon. He has published more than thirty books and numerous articles in several languages. Chryssavgis lives in Maine.

Tim DeChristopher is a climate activist and co-founder of Climate Disobedience Center and of Peaceful Uprising. He became nationally known in 2008 after an act of civil disobedience to stop a Bureau of Land Management oil and gas auction in Utah, for which he spent two years in federal prison. His story was told in the film *Bidder 70* and has been featured in a wide variety of national and international media. DeChristopher received his Master of Divinity degree from Harvard Divinity School and currently works as a hospital chaplain in Rhode Island.

Natasha DeJarnett is the research coordinator at National Environmental Health Association (NEHA) where she leads research, as well as children's environmental health activities. She is a graduate of the University of Louisville in Kentucky, where she completed her PhD and Masters of Public Health degrees concentrating in environmental health sciences. In her postdoctoral studies, she was awarded a fellowship by the National Institute of Environmental Health Sciences to investigate cardiovascular risks of air pollution exposures. DeJarnett was named 2017 Alumna of the Year for the University of Louisville School of Public Health and Information Sciences and was concurrently awarded designation in the class of 2017 Alumni Fellows. Prior to NEHA, she was a policy analyst at the American Public Health Association, where she led the Natural Environment portfolio, including air and water exposures along with climate change. DeJarnett is a member of the Governing Board of Citizens' Climate Education.

Gerald L. Durley is pastor emeritus of the historic Providence Missionary Baptist Church of Atlanta, where he served for nearly twenty-five years. Durley's previous roles include executive director of the Head Start Program for Fulton and Douglas Counties, director of the Health Promotion Resource Center at the Morehouse School of Medicine, and founder of Perspectives, International, a consortium of historically black colleges and universities. In 2011, Durley was inducted into the International Civil Rights Walk of Fame for his contributions during the Civil Rights Movement of the 1960s. In 2015, he was honored as a White House "Champion of Change" for his efforts to address climate change and environmental injustice. A nationally and internationally sought-after inspirational and motivational speaker, Durley is chair of the board of Interfaith Power & Light, which actively seeks climate solutions in forty states and 22,000 interfaith houses of worship across the United States.

Shoshana Meira Friedman is a rabbi, musician, teacher, and Jewish leader in the climate and social justice movements. She and her husband Yotam Schachter co-wrote the song "The Tide Is Rising," a climate anthem that has been sung in congregations, rallies, and gatherings in the United States, Brazil, and France. After organizing a large, interfaith civil disobedience action by clergy against a pipeline in Massachusetts, she started Clergy Climate Action (https://www.clergyclimateaction.org/), a project of the Climate Disobedience Center, to organize religious leaders to take direct action on climate change. Friedman was ordained by Hebrew College and graduated from Oberlin College with High Honors in Environmental Studies. She is a Henry David Thoreau Scholar, a graduate of the Wexner Graduate Fellowship, and an alumna of JOIN for Justice. Her publications and music can be found at www.rabbishoshana.com. Friedman lives in Boston, Massachusetts, with her husband and son.

Roger S. Gottlieb is professor of philosophy at Worcester Polytechnic Institute and the author or editor of twenty-one books and more than 150 essays on political theory, ethics, environmentalism, religious life, contemporary spirituality, the Holocaust, and disability. Two of his books received Nautilus Book Awards: the short story collection, *Engaging Voices: Tales of Morality and Meaning in an Age of Global Warming* (2012) and *Spirituality: What It Is and Why It Matters* (2012). His two most recent books are *Political and Spiritual: Essays on Religion, Environment, Disability and Justice* (2014) and *Morality and the Environmental Crisis* (2019).

Katharine Hayhoe is an atmospheric scientist and a professor at Texas Tech University. Her research focuses on understanding what climate change means for people and the places where we live. She hosts the PBS Digital Series *Global Weirding*; served as a lead author for the second, third, and fourth *U.S. National Climate Assessments*; and has been named one of *Time Magazine*'s "100 Most Influential People" and *Fortune Magazine*'s "The World's 50 Greatest Leaders." As a scientist and a Christian, her work emphasizes the importance of thinking deeply about the connection between our values and the impacts of a changing climate.

Christina Leaño serves as associate director of the Global Catholic Climate Movement, a worldwide network of more than 800 Catholic organizations and thousands of Catholics bringing Pope Francis's *Laudato Si'* into action for climate justice. For more than twenty years she has provided leadership on social and environmental justice issues, including co-founding the Filipino American Coalition for Environmental Solidarity. Leaño is also a trained meditation teacher and spiritual director drawing upon close to two decades of contemplative practice, including three years in a Catholic Cistercian monastery. She is passionate about exploring the intersection of spirituality and social justice and supporting people's spiritual transformation through contemplative practices and engagement in social and ecological justice. Leaño holds degrees from Yale University and the Graduate Theological Union. In her free time, she loves forest bathing with her partner Steffano and daughter Malaya Clare.

Mordechai Liebling is founder and director of the Social Justice Organizing Program at the Reconstructionist Rabbinical College in Philadelphia, Pennsylvania. His course "Rabbi as Environmental Activist" was selected as one of the seven best environmental-related classes in all U.S. seminaries. He was executive vice president of Jewish Funds for Justice, and before that, executive director of the Jewish Reconstructionist Federation. Liebling serves on and facilitates the steering committee of Green Justice Philly, a coalition of more than twenty environmental, community, and labor groups. He is considered one of the founders of the contemporary Jewish environmental movement. Liebling has published articles in a wide range of magazines and chapters in several books. He answered the clergy calls to go to Ferguson, Standing Rock, and Charlottesville, and has been arrested numerous times for civil disobedience related to climate change and other issues of social justice.

Cynthia Moe-Lobeda has lectured or consulted in Africa, Asia, Australia, Europe, Latin America, and North America in theology and ethics and matters of climate justice and climate racism, moral agency, globalization, economic justice, public church, eco-feminist theology, and faith-based resistance to systemic oppression. Her book *Resisting Structural Evil: Love as Ecological-Economic Vocation* (2013) won a Nautilus Award for social justice. She also is author of *Healing a Broken World: Globalization and God* (2002), *Public Church: For the Life of the World* (2004), and numerous articles and chapters. She is co-author of *Saint Francis and the Foolishness of God* (1993, 2015), *Say to This Mountain: Mark's Story of Discipleship* (1996), and *The Bible and Ethics: A New Conversation* (2018). Moe-Lobeda is a professor of Christian Ethics at Pacific Lutheran Theological Seminary, Church Divinity School of the Pacific, and the Graduate Theological Union in Berkeley. She holds a PhD from Union Theological Seminary, affiliated with Columbia University.

Corina Newsome serves on the steering committee of Young Evangelicals for Climate Action. Recently transitioning from her career as a zookeeper, she is currently a graduate biology student at Georgia Southern University, specializing in avian conservation. Newsome earned her BA in Zoo and Wildlife Biology from Malone University (Ohio) in 2015. As an undergraduate, she served as the student director for Multicultural Student Services, founded a student-led wildlife outreach education program, and, since graduating, has founded and directed several programs to encourage socioeconomic- and ethnic-minority high school students to consider careers in wildlife science. Newsome grew up in the urban center of Philadelphia and has always had a desire to participate in, and advocate for, the protection of wildlife and natural spaces. Her goal is to encourage minorities in the United States to explore the great outdoors and draw a connection for Christians between their faith and participation in Creation stewardship.

Jay O'Hara is a Quaker who was part of the team that in 2016 shut down five pipelines carrying crude oil from Canada's tar-sands. A visionary climate activist, O'Hara works to deepen the spiritual underpinnings of powerful action in the world. In 2015 he helped lead a pipeline pilgrimage across Massachusetts and New Hampshire against the Kinder Morgan Pipeline. In 2013 he and friend Ken Ward blockaded a 40,000-ton shipment of coal to the Brayton Point power plant in Somerset, Massachusetts. He travels in itinerant gospel ministry within the Religious Society of Friends (Quakers) and is a co-founder of the Climate Disobedience Center.

Kiran Oommen grew up in Eugene, Oregon, and now lives in Washington State, where he studied sociology at Seattle University. He is a plaintiff on the federal climate change lawsuit *Juliana v. United States*, represented by Our Children's Trust. He is also on the board of directors of the Civil Liberties Defense Center, an activist, defense-oriented, law nonprofit. Oommen's mother is a minister in the United Church of Christ, and he grew up in that church community, regularly involving himself in environmental and human rights activism from an early age. Alongside community organizing, Oommen is part of the folk punk collective known as Geophagia, performing political punk music and booking concerts at their DIY venue.

Leah D. Schade is assistant professor of Preaching and Worship at Lexington Theological Seminary in Kentucky. An ordained minister in the Evangelical Lutheran Church in America since 2000, Leah has served congregations in rural, urban, and suburban settings. She earned her MDiv and PhD degrees from Lutheran Theological Seminary–Philadelphia (now United Lutheran Seminary). Schade has served as an anti-fracking and climate activist, community organizer, and advocate for environmental justice issues. She is the author of *Creation-Crisis Preaching: Ecology, Theology, and the Pulpit* (2015) and *Preaching in the Purple Zone: Ministry in the Red-Blue Divide* (2019). Schade is the "EcoPreacher" blogger for Patheos.com: http://www.patheos.com/blogs/ecopreacher/.

Fred Small has been cited by Bill McKibben as "one of the key figures in the religious environmental surge." A Unitarian Universalist parish minister for nearly two decades, Fred is also a singer-songwriter and environmental lawyer. In 2015, he left parish ministry to devote his energies to climate advocacy, serving as Minister for Climate Justice at Arlington Street Church, Boston. One of the first to engage in civil disobedience to draw attention to climate change, he was arrested with twenty-one others in prayer outside the U.S. Department of Energy in Washington, D.C., in May 2001. In March

2007, he was a lead organizer of the Interfaith Walk for Climate Rescue from Northampton to Boston. *Grist Magazine* named him one of "15 Green Religious Leaders" worldwide.

Tink Tinker is a citizen of the Osage Nation and an elder in the urban American Indian community of Denver. He is the Clifford Baldridge Emeritus Professor of American Indian Cultures and Religious Traditions at Iliff School of Theology, where he taught for thirty-four years. His seminars covered American Indian cultures, history, and religious traditions; postcolonial thought; and justice and peace studies. Tinker holds an MDiv degree from Pacific Lutheran Theological Seminary and a PhD from the Graduate Theological Union. Author of nearly one hundred journal articles, he also authored several books, including *American Indian Liberation: A Theology of Sovereignty* (2008), *Spirit and Resistance: Political Theology and American Indian Liberation* (2004), and *Missionary Conquest: The Gospel and Native American Genocide* (1993). He is co-editor of *Native Voices: American Indian Identity and Resistance* (2003). A Lutheran by maternal heritage, he also served as an editor on *The Peoples' Bible* project. Tinker has volunteered in the Indian community as (nonstipendiary) director of Four Winds American Indian Council in Denver for twenty-five years. In that capacity he has functioned as a traditional American Indian spiritual leader and continues to work closely with the American Indian Movement of Colorado.

Peterson Toscano describes himself as a "quirky, queer Quaker" and draws on comedy, storytelling, and history to create original content for the stage, the Internet, and radio. He seeks to inspire curiosity about climate change while motivating people to discover their roles on this new planet. As the host of Citizens' Climate Radio and the curator of Climate Stew (https://climatestew.com/), he takes a serious look at global warming without scaring the snot out of you. His live presentations reveal the interconnectedness of power, privilege, justice, polar bears, and coffee beans. Some of these presentations include, *Everything Is Connected—An Evening of Stories, Most Weird, Many True*; *Climate Change—What's Faith Got to Do, Got to Do with It?*; and *Climate Change and the Art of Storytelling*. Toscano's website is www.petersontoscano.com.

Lennox Yearwood Jr., president and CEO of Hip Hop Caucus, is a Church of God in Christ Elder and a community activist. Hip Hop Caucus is a national, nonprofit, nonpartisan organization that engages and empowers young people and communities of color in the political process. The organization has registered and mobilized tens of thousands of young voters to vote at the polls. After Hurricane Katrina in 2005, Yearwood established the award-winning Gulf Coast Renewal Campaign, leading a coalition of national and grassroots organizations to advocate for the rights of Katrina survivors. In 2010, Yearwood was named one of the 100 most powerful African Americans by *Ebony Magazine*, and one of the "10 Game Changers in the Green Movement" by the *Huffington Post*. He is the subject of a Discovery Network Documentary, *Hip Hop Rev*. Yearwood co-hosts *Think 100%: The Coolest Show on Climate Change*, an award-winning weekly podcast and live radio show focused on storytelling and sharing just solutions to climate change.